P9-CMO-260

The Ex-Candidate

by

Ned Snead

Dedicated To All The Women In My Life—
I can't afford to list them all for two reasons:
I might offend someone by leaving her out;
and if by chance the list were complete,
it might raise some embarrassing questions.

Contents

Introduction To The Ex-Candidate

After Christmas 1987 things got quiet enough for me to enjoy the visiting water birds at my home on Lake Buchanan. My financial affairs were in good shape, and my business was running well with almost no attention from me. My kids were all educated, married, and scattered where one atom bomb couldn't get them all. I was in love with a charming new wife. Things couldn't get much better.

Then I read a book celebrating the 200th year of the United States Constitution and became disturbed at how far our present system of government has strayed from the original plan. It occurred to me that it was *my job* to straighten out all the silliness and insanity I had been complaining about to my beer drinking buddies.

I had written several letters to Senator Lloyd Bentsen with a great idea to end the cold war, make productive use of thousands of intercontinental ballistic missiles, and produce electric power without pollution and greenhouse gasses. At first I received form letter replies, and then one that obviously came from Bentsen himself saying, "We can't out-spend the Soviets."

Bentsen was up for re-election the next year, and suddenly I got the idea that it was time to carry my great ideas straight to Congress. Surely the people of Texas were ready for a bright new voice in the Senate, and I would promise not to ask for more than one term. I would retire from public service at the age of 65 after having done my bit to clean up the mess in Washington.

Sherron laughed when I first mentioned it to her, but she is a political creature. Her uncle, Preston Smith, had been governor of Texas, and her parents had worked for him while he was in office. The next thing I knew she had hired a campaign manager and arranged for me to announce my bid at a press conference in the State Capitol.

The next three months were wild. We travelled all over Texas to hand out cards and make three-minute speeches anywhere Republicans would listen. There were three other candidates for the nomination. Two were fairly well-known politicians, and the other was a businessman who spent more than twice as much of his own money as I did. Mercifully, I got my honorable discharge early. Two others had to continue campaigning in a run-off for the privilege of being beaten easily by Lloyd Bentsen in the general election.

Mine may have been the shortest political career of all time. For a couple of years Sherron and I attended the Republican gatherings and gave money to the candidates. I still had a powerful urge to tell people how to solve the big problems, so I began writing a series of Ex-Candidate's Reports. Some of them were published by the *Williamson County Sun, The Georgetown Weekly,* and the *Brady Standard/Herald*, owned by Sherron's parents.

Later on we invested some money in an effort to keep the *Austin Weekly* in business. As the publisher continued to need more cash to keep going, he hit on the idea of appealing to my vanity. Eventually I was called every week to be sure I had written something for the "Publisher's Perspective." The editor did me a favor by sometimes deciding not to print what I had written and other times by leaving out or cleaning up the stuff that would have gotten me on somebody's hit list. Even with the editor's help I prompted several nasty letters and alienated some of the advertisers. My little adventure as a publisher ended up costing me more than my political campaign.

The disease is in remission now. This little book is not intended to correct all the problems of the world. Only my kids and my friends will receive copies, and they will not be required to read it.

Thanks for staying with me this far. I hope you enjoy the rest of the book.

Edwin deS. (Ned) Snead
February 1995

Edwin deS. (Ned) Snead

Ned Snead Interview On WOAI

"One of the people who is running for State Board of Education is Ned Snead, and he's with us right now. Ned Snead, welcome to the Carl Wigglesworth Show and good to have you here today."

Ned: Thank you, Carl.

Carl: In past experience in the teaching profession, what makes you want to run for State Board of Education?

Ned: Well, Carl, I think you've got your notes screwed up. I'm running for the U.S. Senate.

Carl: Oh, they have you down here as district 5, State Board of Education.

Ned: Well, I'm Ned Snead, Republican candidate for the U. S. Senate.

Carl: All right, OK, they did give me the wrong information.

Ned: OK, well, maybe I can help you out a little bit.

Carl: Well, all right, we can switch to that because we have also had the, ah, an opponent of yours on, Beau Boulter, about a week ago, who is also running for that seat, correct?

Ned: Yes, he is. He's a good man but I don't believe he can beat that Democrat that's in the office now.

Carl: All right, he's going to be running against Lloyd Bentsen if he wins, and so will you, right?

Ned: Right.

Carl: So you're competing for the same spot on the Republican ticket on Super Tuesday.

Ned: That's right.

Carl: OK give me Ned Snead. Let me shift gears here with a different set of questions. U.S. Senate. Lloyd Bentsen. As you said Beau Boulter would have a hard time beating him. I must say equally you would have a hard time beating him too, would you not?

Ned: Oh, I don't expect it to be easy. I'm an engineer and a businessman. I'm not a lawyer, and I have promised that I will never be a career politician.

Carl: And, why are you running then. What is it you are looking for, what do you want to do?

Ned: Well, I have been accumulating messages for Congress for quite a few years now, and I can't get 'em to answer my letters or my phone calls, so I just decided to carry the message there in person.

Carl: You say, "Carry the message there in person", what message do you want to take?

Ned: Well, I've got quite a number of them. I think the Congressmen and Senators should be limited to two terms in office just like the president is. Break up the seniority system. Of course, like all Republicans, I think we need a Constitutional amendment demanding a balanced budget every year unless we are in a war declared by Congress. But, ah, those are the ordinary things. I'm pretty much a long-range, far-out thinker, rather than inclined, as I think my opponents are, toward band-aid quick fixes for the immediate problems.

Carl: All right, then, give us some of the things you are actually proposing. What do you want to do. I mean the generalities sound nice, but I can get any Democrat, any Republican, anybody else to say they would solve all our problems for us.

Ned: Now, I didn't tell you to say that, did I?

Carl: OK, ha ha, well what do you say? What specifically would you try to get done, realizing you have to work with the rest of the US Senate?

Ned: Well, I'd like to get every boy and girl in the USA to devote his eighteenth year to his country in military service for one thing. And not a matter of draft. I don't think the unlucky ought to serve. I think everyone ought to serve so the next war is everybody's war. But I do believe that in order to keep the peace you have to stay ready for war. On the other hand I feel like forty years of mutual assured destruction is enough for me and you too. I think it's time to start very cautious cooperation with the Soviets on the problems that face all mankind.

Carl: You approve of the INF treaty and President Reagan's moves in that direction?

Ned: Yes, I do. I think he's done a beautiful job with one exception. I don't care much for the idea of crushing and burning these things, because I don't believe the observers are gonna know a dummy or a dud from a really poisonous rocket. So I would recommend the simplest case would be to just take the warheads off and into some one square mile target area in the deepest part of the Atlantic Ocean. That way anything that blew up on the launching ramp or couldn't hit the target would get no credit. It would be very easy to keep track, and I've never been convinced that we are going to be able to allow Soviet generals to crawl all over the United States looking for anything that interests them, and they're not going to do the same for us. But something like this would give us a really workable verification system.

Carl: You don't believe the one that has been negotiated so far is workable?

Ned: Oh, I doubt it. I think it's going to be very expensive, and I don't think it's going to prove.....I don't think it's reliable.

Carl: OK. Let me get to one that I believe is concerning more Americans than INF treaties and nuclear destruction and that is our own pocketbooks. The American economy, in particular the Texas economy I'm sure you know is not in it's best shape ever. The whole American economy, I think every economist agrees, has huge clouds on the horizon....a lot of ideas as to how to make it through the storm....

Ned: Well, I think we need to get a bunch of Texans working again, I have a proposal to build an interstate railway system for 200-mile-per-hour trains like the French and the Japanese have.

Carl: 200-mile-per-hour trains between where and where?

Ned: Well, we are working on an initial deal that would run from Fort Worth to San Antonio, but eventually would like to run it all the way from Amarillo down to McAllen, and then take in Houston and El Paso. But I want to emphasize that I don't want the taxpayers to pay for this. I want this to be a toll road financed by private investors. I think they ought to start buying the land right now while it's cheap, and then... incidentally, the same right or way could be used for150-mile-per-hour cars and busses as long as we have cheap gasoline. But, uh....

Carl: So you're suggesting making like the Autobahns of Europe over here....

Ned: Except faster and with more discipline. I would like to have the cars especially designed and in communication with the dispatchers so that anyone who misbehaves would immediately be identified and have his license removed.

Carl: OK, well, they don't seem to have much problem with that in Europe.

Ned: No, they work pretty good, but they don't go quite as fast as I think they ought to go here. I think they .....the Autobahns were designed forty years ago.

Carl: Of course all these things are based on what technology is available and the price tag that goes with it. I know they can make 150-mile-per-hour cars. We already have some, but most of them cost around $30,000 and more.

Ned: I'd say thirty thousand probably wouldn't get it for you. But on the other hand, look at it this way. If it got from San Antonio to Dallas in an hour and a half or something like that, you'd have the advantage of the same rig.....you would not have to rent a car. You could go directly from your house to the speedway. Off the speedway go directly to your destination, and for the first few years when these cars are rare, I can't imagine a better way to pick up girls.

(Long pause, laughter....)

Carl: "Pick up girls" ha ha. Now I'm wondering, are you really a serious candidate for the US Senate?

Ned: You bet I am. I am as serious as I can be. I'm having a little trouble getting attention for these far-out ideas, you know.

Carl: Yeah, I'd say yes, you do have some far-out ideas. 150-mile-per-hour cars, uh, I mean some day I'm sure that's gonna be possible and practical.

Ned: I think we can start now, and I think it will put 20,000 Texans to work.....

Carl: And you use a lot of terms like you think they should start buying this right of way today, but who's the "they" that's going to buy it?

Ned: I have a theory that as long as you build the frontage road first, a speedway or whatever you want to call it, actually adds to the value of the land to a depth of about a thousand feet on each side. So if it only doubles the value, then the land owner has about a four to one pay-off even before the road is built.

Carl: All right, but, to get this you have to change the laws passed by Congress, because they won't even allow you to have an expressway like that.

Ned: That's right.

Carl: This is not a free country for those kind of ideas.

Ned: What I plan to do is to put some of my people to work, regardless of how this election comes out, trying to get options to buy this right of way. Then before we go to the Legislature or to Congress we are going to have a stack of contracts. We'll say all we want is for the government to get out of the way and let the productive people get to work on this. And I'm as serious as I can be about this. I'd like for you to see one of the little tabloids I have put together describing this project.

Carl: All right, that's one of the things that you would do, and we'll get to some of the others. His name is Ned Snead. He's running for United States Senate, Republican primary against Beau Boulter and about three or four other candidates which we'll have on the radio this week before Super Tuesday. Of course, you can ask Ned Snead your questions too. The number is 737-1200. If you live outside San Antonio, dial 1-737-1234.

(music and commercials)

Carl: Carl Wigglesworth on WOAI radio. Can't stay at the Motel Six if you're doing 150 though, you pass them pretty quick. The gentleman is running for United States Senate, Republican primary, Super Tuesday. Ned Snead is his name. He says one of the solutions to the economy of Texas would be a SUPER highway and train.... 200-mile-per-hour trains, 150-mile-per-hour cars going from Amarillo down to the Valley....San Antonio, Fort Worth, Houston, Dallas area. So that would take in a pretty big part of the state. What happened to El Paso? Why no highways from here to there? That would seem like a natural too.

Ned: Well, I see that as phase two. As a matter of fact we have another plan to come from El Paso, south of Midland, San Angelo, on through the center of the state, a little north of Houston and Beaumont, so that we'd be tying Texas together both east-west and north-south.

Carl: I take it that you are familiar with the highway that is already funded. The people are already committed to doing it, but the United States government is not allowing them to do it in Colorado. The front range super highway, and all they propose is a very modest 100-mile-per-hour highway between Colorado Springs and the Wyoming border I believe.....maybe Pueblo, Colorado and the Wyoming border.....a stretch of three hundred miles, and they can't get Congress to approve the rights to do it.

Ned: So that's why we've got to send some new people to Congress.

Carl: OK, Marcel, you're on WOAI.

Marcel: Uh, I've got about two questions for you sir. One thing.....my car won't go over 85 miles per hour. That's number one. I'd have to sell my car and get another car that would go 150.

Carl: Well, if you want to drive on that highway. No one forces you to drive on this super speedway.

Marcel: Right, right. The other question I have. He's talking about the Autobahn. The Autobahn is originally designed as a landing strip and takeoff for the Messerschmidts which they hid in a parking area under trees and so forth. And we sort of went around it during the second world war. Because we just thought is was only highways, and it wasn't that really complex, but they were used as landing strips. Uh, uh, the Autobahn was. And they still have police cars which they drive Porche, and they still control the traffic. They're not lettin' anybody go, I don't think 150. Well, they say no speed limit, but....

Carl: Yeah, well, it's true. I was just there last fall, and believe me, cars are doing 130, 140 miles an hour.

Marcel: I know, but, just don't make an error. Ha ha. Don't swerve.

Carl: But they are good drivers, and they have good enforcement of their laws so that everybody drives on the right except those that are going 130.

Marcel: But why should we have such a high speed area even from El Paso to Houston and vice versa?

Ned: Want me to answer that?

Others: Yes.

Ned: I believe that some time in this generation there will be a real shortage of petroleum, and we really should do something smarter than fight over who gets to burn up what's left. Now as I see it the high-speed road is the "sizzle". The "steak" in my opinion is the high-speed train. But I have been convinced that Texans are not yet ready to give up their pickups and gun racks and get on trains. And I don't think the price of fuel is going up very sharply very soon. The real reason for doing this is to go ahead and get the right of way now while the land is lightly settled and when it can be acquired cheaply. Whether we do the 150-mile-per-hour thing or not is really immaterial. The main thing is to get the land now because as Texas builds up we're going to need a fast way to get around, and a train is ten times as efficient in terms of passenger miles per gallon as an airliner. When I came on this thing I was trying to say that my plans are 20 or 30 years out in front.

Marcel: Truthfully, being from Texas, I've been out here thirty five years from New York. I had some property which I bought right past Sea World. This is the truth. And I project myself for ten years, and as of today it's thirty five years. So to that respect I think you're right, truthfully. Because this land has to be appropriated now for future use. There's no getting around it, and if we don't do it now like you say, truthfully, I don't care if it's 150 or whatever it is, the land has to be appropriated so there is access to any part of Texas, or anywhere in the United States.

Ned: And in order to go FAST on this road we are not going to be able to use existing railroad right of ways. We're gonna have to have curves with a minimum radius of about two and a half miles. It's gotta be all new. We've gotta go through virgin territory, through the farm and ranch land.

Marcel: Well, I'm only sixty two, and I don't want to go 150 miles an hour.

Ned: Well, I'm fifty eight, and I'm probably gonna have a co-pilot driving me around.

Carl: All right, thank you, Marcel. Jerome, your turn. You're on WOAI, and you're talking to Ned Snead. Go ahead.

Jerome: First of all, just a little pun. Yeah, now, Mr. Snead, you will need a co-pilot out there if you're gonna have little girls going there between San Antonio and Amarillo. First of all you might wind up the way Gary Hart did. But that isn't what I'm really concerned with. I work, and I'm the same age as the other gentleman was. Grew up in Texas. Yellow dog, straight line, straight ticket Democrat, OK? And I have voted for years Republican to establish a two-party system. And we are being rather successful with it. But when the national committee comes in and says, "If you lose the election to Fox or Gilbreath, there is no support from the national committee, and only Beau is gonna get one-point-one million", it seems to me that there is something remiss to the contenders that are opposed to Beau that is not being brought out. We are being blackmailed with one-point-one million dollars to vote against you.

Ned: (laughing) I have been assured by the committee that handles this million dollars that they will stay neutral. So I think Beau has started counting his chickens before they hatch. But that's not going to be enough anyway. We're going to have to.....In order to unseat the democrats, we're going to have to get the money from the ordinary voters. The entrenched politicians at the top of these powerful committees can get all the money they need from....the lobbyists. If we're really gonna have a real election, we're gonna have to start getting the five and ten dollar contributions from the people who have had enough of the tax-and-spend type of democratic government.

Jerome: You're correct there, and you're gonna need an awful lot of people that....I talk to Knox Duncan on this thing and got nowheres, and he's almost convinced me to, Hey, go back where I came from on, Hey, being a yellow-dog democrat. Sorry, Sir, but that's what you run into with the establishment. This is true not only in the Republican but it's also true in the Democrat party.

Ned: If you'll put me in that general election, I am a fairly wealthy man myself, and I think I've got enough seed money to bring in what it's gonna take to beat 'em. I also think that, to some extent, the election is going to be determined by what the Soviets do and what the economy does.....that it's not gonna be all determined by money. You know, you cannot BUY an election. At some point that money comes back to haunt you.

Jerome: I'd like to say one more thing, and I'll let you go, Carl. The other day Carl had a....a political analyst, and he said the opposite. The reason the national committee can command the attention they're doing with the power they have is.....money. So what that political analyst was saying on Carl's show the other day is that it's money that determines the elections, and us people that are trying to establish a two-party system.....we're just kinda out there.... gonna have to fight and claw 'till we win....over.... money.

Ned: Keep in mind that not more than about twenty per cent of the people are settling these elections. So if you really want to fight and claw, you can get out there and find out who agrees with you and get them to vote. And you are the kind of people I'm counting on.

Carl: Thank you for the ideas and comments. 737-1200 is the number. Ned Snead is running for United States Senate in the Republican primary. He's on the ballot on Super Tuesday, and we'll find out more about why he thinks you should vote for him right after news and weather update.

(commercials, etc.)

Carl: His name is Ned Snead. He's running for United States Senate on the Republican side of things for the primary coming up Super Tuesday. 737-1200 is telephone number, and long distance, you're calling from Austin, go right ahead.

Voice: Well, Hello

Carl: Hello.

Voice: The question I want to raise is consideration of the repeal of the drug prohibition. The reason for raising the question and trying to get this on the agenda is: we have just been treated over this weekend to a call by the state and county government to spend more tax money to build more jails here in Texas in spite of the fact that, according to the Bureau of Justice statistics in 1981, we were putting less than the national average per capita in the jails, that rate per capita went up 50 per cent, and we are now over the national average. And on further investigation, we find that about a third of our criminal justice system in Texas, the jail system, about a third of it, at a conservative estimate, is being consumed by this idiotic effort to socialize personal responsibility. It doesn't work. It's corrupting our government, and the policy seems to be corrupting....has already corrupted several governments throughout Latin America. Do you have any ideas on how to address this problem?

Ned: I sure do. Carl, did you put that guy on there just for my benefit?

Carl: No, I didn't.

Ned: What's his name?

Voice: Terry Liberty Parker in Austin.

Ned: Terry?

Carl: Terry Parker in Austin, Texas.

Ned: Parker. I believe our war on drugs is gettin' nowhere. I believe that three-time convicted drug dealers should get an overdose of their own merchandise. And then, in addition, I feel like if we're gonna give away clean needles to stop the spread of AIDS, we might as well give away the dope to go in 'em. At least the dope fiends would not have to rob and steal to support their habit. So I probably agree with you better than anybody else.

Terry: Could be. Uh, by the way, Rider Scott on your station, not on your program, Carl, but on your station, Rider Scott on the general council for the governor seemed to indicate that the difference between the legal price of cocaine and the black market price of cocaine was five dollars an ounce versus ten dollars an ounce, and of course he couldn't see how that would make any difference on the crime rate. In fact the difference is this. The Sigma Chemical Company legally sells cocaine to those who are authorized to buy it, and this is the same stuff that's called crack on the street, for seven dollars a gram. On the street it's a hundred and fifty dollars a gram. An ordinary person has no other way to sustain that habit but to go out and steal six hundred dollars worth of merchandise every day in order to fence it for a fourth of its worth. That means it's not a wonderful life for the addict, to be an addict, but we're compounding the problem with this echo from the old alcohol prohibition by having these addicts come out and terrorize the rest of us, stealing our stereos, and we're corrupting our government, and uh, with these enormous black market profits.

Carl: All right, a comment from our candidate.

Ned: Well I wish I had him along to campaign with me. He could just as well make my speech.

Carl: OK. Thank you for calling from Austin. On the mobile line, Ray, you're on WOAI. Go ahead.

(confusion due to auto radio & mobile phone)

Ray: Yes the gentlemen called a little while ago. He wanted the two-party system.... that's why he was backing the Republicans, and I'm saying to him that if that's the case then we don't need another Republican, because we have a Democrat and a Republican Senator, and maybe what we need to have is to keep it like that instead of having two Republicans. I think that with two Republicans we need two Republicans like we need a head in the hole.

Carl: A hole in the head. The message is plain, yes. Go ahead.

Ned: I have a suspicion that this guy who just called in is not a Republican. Incidentally I asked your buddy over there if I could speak a little Spanish on the air. Can I do that?

Carl: Well, very little, 'cause I can't keep up with you if you start that.

Ned: Does the fellow on the phone speak Spanish?

Carl: He's already hung up.

Ned: OK....tell him that,"Mucha gente creen que las personas que hablan espanol no votaran para un republicano, pero los amigos mios que hablan espanol han trabajado por toda la vida y no estan buscando algo gratis. Quieren exacatamente lo que quieren todo el mundo....la opportunidad, lo que es justo, y respecto."

Carl: Ah, you want to translate that for us, Mr. Snead?

Ned: Well, I just said that people tell me that people who speak Spanish won't vote for a Republican, all of my friends who speak Spanish have been working hard all their lives, and they're not looking for somethin' for nothin', and that, uh, they just want opportunity, justice and respect.

Carl: And our guest is Ned Snead. He's running for United States Senate in the Republican primary on Super

Tuesday. You can talk to him, too. We have a couple of lines open. The number 737-1200. If you live outside San Antonio, dial 1-737-1234. I say something truly amazing the other day. I heard these were coming

(he continues with a commercial for color copiers)

Carl: Carl Wigglesworth. He's running for U.S. Senate on the Republican ticket. Ned Snead is his name, and you are talking to him. Go ahead.

Voice: Thank you. Ah, one comment. The gentlemen who called in, the man immediately in front and the other man who is a democrat.....voted Republican. I think in a very broad sense they're saying the same thing, that they want a two-party system and not a complete democrat or a complete republican. Going back to what you were saying about your transportation, Mr. Snead. You might be, have been, uh, twenty to thirty years ahead. Why don't you jump a little further and talk about monorails? That's the....they're more efficient. They're safer. They've proven theirself. We already have the technology....in the world. I don't think we have it over here. But if you think about that.... your right of ways and everything else.... should diminish.

Ned: My concern is not for any particular mode of transportation. My concern is to, right now, while Texas is lightly settled, and while the land is cheap, that we acquire the right of way for some type of high-speed transportation. I have no objection at all if monorail turns out to be the most technically feasible. I also have no objection to magnetic levitation and other things that have been proposed. But I figure that it's hard enough to get people to take me seriously, so I stick to proven technologies like the French and the Japanese. But I agree with you, there's nothing wrong with monorail.

Voice: I understand why you..... because people can relate to proven technology. But we have been dormant, ignorant, ears closed, lacking of (?) something as far as monorails go. But it is just too great a transportation system, that uh, is just being ignored. I appreciate it, and thank you.

Ned: Well, you're gonna' vote for me anyway?

Carl: Larry, you're on WOAI.

Larry: Mr. Snead, sir.

Ned: Yes sir.

Larry: Ah, I'd like to hear some more of your comments about the military and uh, bringing back the draft did you say?

Ned: No, I particularly don't like the draft, because I, I have the feeling that a draftee is an unlucky guy who has to go do a dirty job while somebody else stays home and goes to graduate school or something. I would have it universal. I would have it, every boy and every girl put in at least a year in military training and then if they want to do Peace Corps or missionary work or almost anything else, uh, they could do that too. But I particularly want the white-collar warriors in Washington to know that it may be their kid or their grandson that goes to the next war that they declare.

Larry: As an ex veteran, sir, I wholeheartedly agree that everybody should at least serve in the military in some way, shape, or form, be it National Guard, Reserve, Army, Navy, Air Force, Marines, Coast Guard, something. (confusion) They should give back something of what this country has given to them.

Ned: I totally agree with you. I served in the Korean War, and uh, I think a lot of civilians don't realize how few military personnel ever get shot at. I was over there for a year with a war going on all around me, and as far as I know, nobody ever shot at me personally. But there's thousands and thousands of jobs to be done, and well, (laughter) I think it's everybody's job.

Carl: All right, Larry, thank you, and our guest is Ned Snead running for U S Senate, Republican primary on Super Tuesday. The number 737-1200 here at WOAI.

(commercial)

Carl: Carl Wigglesworth on WOAI radio and our guest is Ned Snead, running for U S Senate. We have a caller who is not on the line but wanted to know how he could contribute to your campaign. He says he likes what he hears.

Ned: Boy, am I glad to hear that. The mailing address is post office box six, Georgetown, and you'd be amazed how hard it is to raise money for a campaign this year.

Carl: OK, box six, Georgetown, Texas, and zip code is?

Ned: 78626

(Note: P. O. Box 6 was rented only for the campaign)

Carl: 78626 All right, let's see, next caller on the line is Stan. You're on WOAI radio, go ahead.

Stan: Good afternoon, Carl, uh, Mr. Snead.

Ned: Yes, sir, Stan.

Stan: Senator Bentsen, along with others in Congress, gave away the Panama Canal. It is of vital interest to the United States, both economically and from the standpoint of our national security. How would you propose to deal with this situation?

Ned: Well, I'm glad you asked, because I have been thinking about it. It ties in with another item. I've been in Guatemala and Belize and Brazil, but I've never been in Nicaragua. I doubt that our taxpayers' money is gonna be able to dislodge a well-entrenched government, so I'd be more inclined to export prosperity to Nicaragua than political instability. Long ago plans were made to dig a sea-level canal across Nicaragua, which would let our aircraft carriers and the escorts operate in two oceans without making a ten-day trip around Cape Horn. So I'd like to make the same kind of treaty we made in Panama 90 years ago. Then I'd have every engineer and construction man be required to be fluent in Spanish and buy all his supplies locally. If possible, I's rather overwhelm the locals with prosperity and tourists, than ...of course, we's have our own naval and air bases there to look after our own interests. I think Panama could eventually become just a tourist route for millionaires' yachts.

Carl: OK, thank you, Stan. Mary Jane, you're on WOAI.

Mary: Good afternoon. Uh, I want to tell Mr. Snead I am what you call a Spanish-speaking American, and I was born in Litton Springs, Texas, and I agree with him. We're not, uh, we don't want free stuff. We just want a chance to make a living, and he is a real swell fellow. The only thing I sorry is that on Channel 41 last night, or last afternoon, a Mr. Duncan talked and said a lot of things that is gonna change a lot of Spanish-speaking people, you know.

Carl: Duncan Knox, Republican Party Chairman in this area.

Mary: Uh huh, he called the Spanish-speaking people, the ones that don't know English, you know, the old ones, and maybe some new ones, that have crossed over, you know, short from stupid and all that.

Carl: Well, that wouldn't be very wise politically for sure. Mary Jane, I need to cut it a little bit short because we have 30 seconds for our guest to wrap it up here for today. People should vote for you on Super Tuesday coming up, Ned Snead, because basically you're gonna get government off their backs?

Ned: Well, that's one of the things. I'd like to answer Mary Jane. Incidentally language, I think, is a trade barrier to most Americans. I think we ought to call an international convention to select a trade language for all the world and teach it to all children from their first year in school. That would be in addition to their native language. But getting back to why you should vote for me, my uncle, M. J. Neeley said he would never hire a man who likes to fish or play golf. Well, that's part of my platform. Just remember Ned Snead is the yodeling Senator who's too busy to play golf.

Carl: All right, Ned Snead, thank you for being here today. We are out of time. Primary day is Super Tuesday coming up a week from tomorrow. Thank you for being with us.

The Ex-Candidate

Losing An Election

March 18, 1988

First, the embarrassment and disappointment of losing an election only lasts for about a day.

Second, there is a tremendous sense of relief that there is no more campaigning to be done, and no need to take on a public job with no simple answers and no possibility of satisfying all the people who would demand your attention.

Third, is the appearance of so many friends and supporters, and the newly acquired skills of reaching out to strangers.

During the campaign there is a tremendous sense of urgency and importance in every hour. The old, every day sense of meaninglessness is overwhelmed by a passion to get the TRUTH to everybody. The candidate knows without a doubt that he is doing the Lord's work. Campaigning is LIVING at the peak of intensity.

Obviously, running for office is not for everybody, but it's too important to be left to lawyers and politicians. Any one who has a reason to complain about the government should consider taking an active part in it.

But if you think of public office as a means to personal gain, forget it. The pay is too low, the hours too long, and the cost of getting the job may be twenty times the salary or more. If you get in it for the money, you will just be part of the problem.

On the other hand, if you are lucky and clever enough to have lived as long as you have, and to have accumulated more than you need, maybe it's your name that is being called.

To continue living like you have been, you depend on smart and honest governors, legislators, judges, commissioners, mayors, councilmen and party chairmen. The wisdom you have accumulated may be exactly what is needed somewhere, and there is no better way to invest your time and money for the benefit of your children.

If you think you hear your name being called, even faintly, volunteer. It will begin the most exciting time of your life. And if you are really not needed now, the Lord and the people will give you an honorable discharge.

SNEAD FOR U.S. SENATE

Political Advertisement paid for by Vernon Jordan, Treasurer, Post Office Box 6, Georgetown, Texas 78627, Ned Snead for U.S. Senate Campaign

REPUBLICAN PRIMARY

SNEAD FOR SENATE

Political Advertisement paid for by Vernon Jordan, Treasurer, Post Office Box 6, Georgetown, Texas 78627, Ned Snead for U.S. Senate Campaign

TOGETHER, WE CAN DEFEAT LLOYD BENTSEN IN NOVEMBER.

NED SNEAD TALKS ABOUT HIS CANDIDACY

I am seeking the Republican nomination for the United States Senate because I believe our state and our nation need a man from the business world to address the serious economic problems we are facing.

Most Texans don't need a newspaper, radio or television commentator to tell them we have been having hard times for several years in our Lone Star State. What's even worse, the fiscal problems of our nation have become an international embarrassment.

Washington needs new ideas. The worn and tired old ideas have been tried and have failed. If a businessman keeps trying old ideas in a faltering business, he will soon lose that business.

"Of course new ideas are controversial. What did England think of our Declaration of Independence?"

For 35 years I have been in the business of creating jobs—of developing and promoting businesses that have put Texans to work. Every business endeavor in which people joined with me in giving their time, effort and skills has been a success.

New ideas, new approaches, new solutions and new markets—these are the keys to success in business. These are the credentials I offer the voters of Texas.

Some people think that being a newcomer to politics is a liability. Frankly, I can't think of a greater asset. Every statesman started out as a newcomer. Experienced political operatives—not newcomers—have created the mess in government.

There is another fallacy afoot in political circles today. Many think that a candidate acquires credibility by having run for or served in political office before! Name recognition has become more important than a candidate's abilities! Does this sound like the citizen-statesman concept our Founding Fathers had in mind for persons who are to speak for us in the Congress?

When you go to the polls on March 8th, I ask you to consider these thoughts and judge for yourself if these are the ideas and ideals you want of your candidate for the United States Senate.

Ned Snead briefs press in State Capitol building regarding his platform.

NED SNEAD REPUBLICAN FOR U.S. SENATE

SUPER TUESDAY, MARCH 8, 1988 IS A DAY OF DECISION FOR ALL REPUBLICAN PRIMARY CANDIDATES.

Media attention has been focused on the fact that Texans and at least 14 other mostly Southern states will cast primary ballots the same day, March 8, exerting powerful influence on who will represent the two major parties in the Presidential election.

It is also vital to remember that Super Tuesday in Texas is the date Republicans and Democrats will select their party's candidates for every position from U.S. Senate to their county and precinct chairmen.

Texas needs another strong voice of reason in Washington, a problem solver whose history of success was written by hard work and the kind of inventive thinking that made our country the economic showcase of the world.

You can elect a man on Super Tuesday who can beat the Democrats in November. You can elect Ned Snead.

Texas Crushed Stone is shipped all over the country from Georgetown.

SNEAD FOR SENATE

SENATE CANDIDATE ADVOCATES BUSINESS APPROACH TO GOVERNMENT

The entrepreneurial spirit on which this country was founded is exemplified in Ned Snead, candidate for the U.S. Senate. His business accomplishments have brought new jobs to Texans over the last 35 years. His platform is innovative and reflects the foresight needed to resolve current issues now that will otherwise create greater problems for the future.

A Distinguished Student graduate from Texas A&M in Mechanical Engineering with business training from the Harvard School of Business, Snead has a comprehensive background in areas as diverse as construction and mining to computer science and space technology. After completing military service as a Communications Officer in the U.S. Air Force during the Korean War, Snead joined his father's construction firm and was instrumental in returning the business to a profitable financial position. His interests then led him to the computer industry as a salesman for

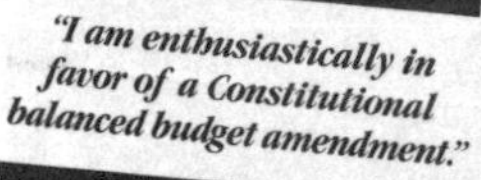

IBM. This experience eventually prompted Snead to form his own business, Snead Management Systems, Houston's oldest software company still in operation. After selling the business, Ned Snead became an inventor, turning his ideas into realities with products needed by industry. Currently, Snead holds 15 foreign and domestic patents which includes the Snead Dump Train, a bulk commodity delivery system, recently leased to Conrail.

Snead has succeeded in every business endeavor he has pursued because he has the ideas and the determination to find workable solutions to challenging problems. He has the strength we need in the U.S. Senate. Vote Snead in the March 8th Primary.

Snead's position on railroads is based on experience. This is an engine on the Georgetown Railroad.

Ned Snead and one of his patented dump trains.

NED SNEAD REPUBLICAN FOR U.S. SENATE

Snead's inventions are "built by and for men with dirt on their boots."

SNEAD PROPONENT FOR INDIVIDUAL LIBERTY

A firm believer that more laws cause a decrease in individual effort and achievement, Snead strongly supports reinstating liberty to the individual and decreasing governmental power. He wants Congress to live by the Constitution. "That document asserted the rights of the individual person in a way the world had never seen before. But almost every law passed in the last 200 years has increased the power of the government and reduced the liberty of the people. I will do all in my power to halt this erosion of personal liberties and eliminate many of the nuisance laws already on the books."

A vote for Ned Snead March 8th will guarantee he has the opportunity to do just that for all of us.

SNEAD FOR SENATE

Ned Snead and his wife Sherron at their home in Georgetown. Together they have five children.

REVITALIZE SPACE EFFORT: SNEAD FOR IT

Republican Ned Snead is an advocate for the revitalization of the space program and believes that the answer to the energy dilemma may be solved in outer space.

If elected to Congress, his main thrust will be toward a commitment of funding research into the use of solar power for energy rather than the use of nuclear or coal powered electricity plants. "If we don't start working to conserve our natural resources, America will become a second class nation."

Ned Snead's proposal of solar collectors orbiting the earth may sound extreme until the numbers are presented. For about $100 billion over the next 30 years, the solar collectors could supply all the electricity needed on earth. According to Snead, $100 billion is less than one-half the annual defense budget and only 15% of what will be spent for coal and nuclear powered electrical generators over the next 30 years.

Snead's energy conservation plans can be linked with President Reagan's recent disarmament treaty with the Soviets. Snead believes efforts should be joined to build a space-based solar power system that could provide inexpensive unlimited power to the world. He supports pooling resources and working towards the goal of space exploration and nuclear disarmament together.

"NASA in partnership with the private sector can develop a sound method to harness solar power."

SNEAD TAKES HARD LINE APPROACH TO WAR ON DRUGS

Ned Snead, candidate for U.S. Senate in the upcoming March 8th Primary, believes in taking a much harder approach to drug abuse than this nation has currently supported.

"Take the profit out of drugs and you stop the pushers."

In order to win the war on drugs, Snead believes severe measures must be enforced if we are ever to see any positive changes.

"We need to either stop allowing jury sentencing and have judges give out established penalties or set up a controlled dispensing system for addicts and eliminate the profit motive in drug dealing. We can kill the business by killing the profit," Snead states.

An accomplished pilot, the Candidate plans to tour Texas, all of it, during his campaign.

VOTE MARCH 8TH IN THE REPUBLICAN PRIMARY

Sherron and Ned Snead prepare to board the campaign train.

VOTE MARCH 8TH FOR NED SNEAD

FREE TRADE ZONE TREATY

The Free Trade Zone Treaty that President Reagan negotiated with Canada was a master stroke for both countries. This treaty eliminates a lot of laws that were barriers to free commerce between these two great countries.

We should pursue the same sort of treaty with Mexico and stimulate growth on both sides of our southern border. This would also be an effective method of alleviating the immigration problem. With new jobs paying better wages on the Mexican side of the border the inclination to pursue better opportunities in the United States would be greatly reduced.

Power Companies Could Lead Us Into 21st Century

Editor's Note: This is a letter the candidate, Mr. Snead wrote before losing the Super Tuesday, March 8, 1988 Republican primary. The remaining writings are as an ex-candidate.

To: Directors and Managers
Electric Generating Utilities

This is an unusual time in history, and it presents some unique opportunities for the electric power industry which may not be repeated soon.

Our Navy is fighting to protect oil for our trading partners.

The promise of nuclear power has lost its public appeal.

Our national effort in space is suffering a crisis in leadership.

We are beginning to suspect that the Soviets want peace.

The Soviets have developed the world's largest spacecraft. (The name is Energia.)

Coal-fired power plants cost twice as much as gas or oil fired plants.

Coal prices are being held up by monopolistic railroad transportation prices.

Environmentalists are worried about carbon dioxide and heat in the atmosphere.

Nearly all practical sites for hydro-electric power in Texas have already been developed.

There are still large areas of unsettled land in the world, particularly Texas and Brazil.

I believe the time has come to form an international co-op of electric utility companies and private investors to begin to develop a ring of Solar Power Satellites.

One of my classmates from Texas A & M, Hubert Davis, who designed the spacecraft that Neil Armstrong and Buzz Aldrin stepped out of onto the moon, was also NASA's chief investigator for the Solar Power Satellite, originally proposed by Dr. Peter Glaser. He concluded that it would work and produce power at a reasonable cost, but the initial investment was far too much to squeeze out of the taxpayers. However, in the thirty years it would take to build, the world's electric utility companies would have to spend seven times as much on nuclear and coal-fired plants to meet the expected demand.

Because the system would release *no* waste gasses and waste heat into the atmosphere, it would make the environmentalists see the utilities as heroes rather than villains.

It would be seen as a thrilling adventure by young people who were aroused by our trips to the moon, but have been disappointed by the recent failures in our space program.

It represents an ideal project for cautious cooperation with the Soviets, friendly competition on a vast scale, and diversion of vast amounts of labor and wealth from dangerous weapons to useful tools for mankind. This is the perfect example of "beating swords into plowshares."

Where can we start? The project is obviously far too large for any one utility company, and perhaps even for a nation which is spending more than its income. The answer is on land.

The last item which will be needed happens to be the first which must be acquired, and the cheapest.

Receiving antennas which convert microwave energy from space into direct current, called *rectennas,* will be built on elliptical areas about five miles in diameter. A forest of devices similar to TV antennas will be supported on an open frame ten or more feet above the ground. Sunlight and rain will fall through, and cattle can graze normally under it.

Birds will fly through the beam without any effect, although airplanes will experience temporary radio interference.

Sites for these receiving antennas must be acquired *now,* while they are still available and cheap. Since they will not need to be occupied for many years, they might be acquired by options with a very small initial cash outlay. At the same time land should be acquired for transformer sites, power lines and service roads to connect the receiving sites to the power grid.

The power companies could signal to the world that they are moving aggressively into the twenty first century just by starting to negotiate for the necessary land.

Another real estate acquisition will be larger and needed sooner. Since about five per cent less fuel is required for rockets launched from the equator, the co-op should acquire a launching area of a hundred square miles or more in the Amazon Valley and fronting on the Atlantic Ocean. This could probably be a gift from the Brazilian government, since their people would expect to supply the site with most of the food, fuel, power, lumber, steel and cement for thousands of technicians working there.

A very low-cost early requirement is the drafting of a charter for the proposed international co-op in English, Russian and Portuguese. Another friend of mine, Art Dula, is a Houston patent attorney familiar with INTELSAT, and who has been negotiating recently with the Soviets on space transportation.

As a first step, I would suggest that your directors and staff plan a seminar discussing the possibilities with Hubert Davis, Art Dula, Peter Glaser and myself.

We may have a unique opportunity to lead the whole world into the twenty-first century.

Sincerely yours,

Ned Snead

On The Panama Canal
March 20, 1988

In the last week of the Republican Senatorial campaign I found a book written in 1977 by Congressman Philip M. Crane entitled, *Surrender In Panama—The Case Against The Treaty.*

The more I read, the madder I became.

The entire text of all the Panama Canal treaties are in the book, including:

Hay-Pauncefote Treaty of 1901—with Britain
Hay-Herran Treaty of 1903—with Colombia
Hay-Bunau-Varilla Treaty of 1903—with Panama
Friendship & Cooperation Treaty of 1936
—with Panama
Treaty of Mutual Understanding & Cooperation
of 1955—Panama
Panama Canal Treaty of 1977—with Panama

The provision which bothers me most is Article XII[2](b) "During the duration of this Treaty, the United States of America shall not negotiate with third states for the right to construct an interoceanic canal on any other route in the Western Hemisphere, except as the two Parties may otherwise agree."

I find it hard to believe that either Jimmy Carter or Lloyd Bentsen have ever read the text of the Treaty they approved. Their days may have been completely filled by official duties, conferences with aides and visitors from home, and by campaigning for the next election. They had to rely on others to tell them that, on balance, the Treaty was acceptable.

In August of 1977 Lloyd Bentsen received 1,889 letters or phone calls with 99 per cent asking him to vote AGAINST the treaty, and yet he voted for it.

I saw Mr. Bentsen in Washington last week and told him that the Panama Canal would be a big issue in this year's general election. He told me that he visited Panama in 1977 and was convinced that failure to ratify the treaty would be playing right into the Castro's hands.

I wonder if a hundred thousand letters from Texans could have stopped him from giving away this extremely valuable national asset which may be essential to the defense of the Western Hemisphere.

However, I don't want to be one who complains without offering a possible solution.

The smartest lawyer I know told me that according to Constitutional Law, a treaty has the same force and effect as an act of Congress, and when two conflict, the most recent overrides the earlier.

Therefore, a bill could be passed by both Houses of Congress and approved by the President to nullify any part of all of the Panama Canal Treaty of 1977. I have personally asked Senators Strom Thurmond and Lloyd Bentsen and Congressman Beau Boulter if they have considered this possibility. Apparently none had, but Mr. Boulter has promised to look into it.

Possibly the old canal is obsolete, being too small for modern supertankers and aircraft carriers, but without it we must have the right to build a larger sea level canal.

I have been excavating rock for 35 years, and my rough estimate for a ditch 1,200 feet wide, 60 feet deep and a hundred miles long would require moving about three billion cubic yards of material. At two dollars per cubic yard, it would cost about six billion dollars, roughly the cost of one aircraft carrier complete with airplanes, but without the fleet of escort ships.

Such a project would bring immense prosperity to Mexico or any Central American country where it might be built. It would also benefit American suppliers of machinery, explosives and tools, and reduce our need for a larger navy.

I have been called a visionary. OK, here is one of my visions, and I want to share it with every Congressman, Senator and challenger in the country. Please, somebody, pick up the ball and run with it.

Written from Panama City

August 10, 1988

Senator Lloyd Bentsen
Hart Building, Room 703
Second and C Streets, N.E.
Washington, D.C. 20510

Dear Mr. Bentsen:

When you visited with Sherron and me in your office in March, I told you that the Panama Canal would be an issue in your campaign. I still believe that, but not in the way I did at that time.

For the last three days, I have been doing my own investigating in Panama. I have read everything I can find and talked to everyone I met, including taxi drivers, canal workers, canal pilots, shipping agents, marine engineers, U.S. State Department employees, and Mr. Julio Noriega, the General's brother and manager of the Commission for Studies of Alternatives to the Panama Canal.

I now believe you were right when you led the Senate to ratify the Treaty of 1977. Although the canal reduces our cost of imported goods and helps us to sell coal and grain overseas, it produces no cash revenue to the U.S. government to offset the 600 million dollars per year we spend here to maintain these United States' presence.

On the other hand, it would be a wonderful opportunity for U.S. leadership and investment in the next generation. The canal is operating at near capacity now and the long term trend shows increasing traffic at an accelerating rate matching the world population growth. Work should be started now to provide a third set of wider and deeper locks and to dredge the upper channel and the approaches for deeper draft ships.

I believe we will be blessed with peace for the rest of this century and we will need to find larger scale, profitable projects for the people and capital no longer needed for war preparation. Here in Panama could be a wonderful opportunity for U.S. investors and workers. All that is needed is a reasonably stable government to protect our investments.

Unfortunately, all that our government has done here in the last year has created instability and ill will toward the United States. Particularly the International Emergency Economic Power Act (IEEPA) imposed here on April 8, 1988 has had no effect on General Noriega or the drug dealers, but has worked great hardship on the middle-class businessman and the poor folks.

This misguided effort is rapidly destroying all the good will you gained by the Treaty of 1977. I hear that people from the East and West (not including the Soviets) are already here preparing to fill the gap when the U.S.A. drops the ball.

We should be working on new profitable deals for the next century with Panama businessmen rather than meddling in their government affairs. As it is, we are making the government stronger and the businessmen weaker, just the opposite of our intentions.

Your good work here is being undone. Please do anything you can to persuade the President to lift this senseless and useless embargo. You were sensitive to the people of Panama ten years ago. Please listen to them now.

Sincerely yours,

Ned Snead
Ex-candidate

Note: Bentsen did not answer this letter.

Political Prophesy: A Third Party
April, 1988

My decision to run for the U.S. Senate was based on many years of being appalled by the silliness and insanity I have seen coming out of the government.

Having been a businessman for thirty five years, I have been particularly repelled by the modern Democrats' desire to take from the rich by force and give to the poor to buy votes. I just naturally assumed that if I were to take part in politics, it would be as a Republican.

When the political virus bit me, I still thought I could see less insanity on the Republican side, and thought I could help them straighten out their act.

Now that I have been bloodied in the political arena, I have far less confidence in my ability to change things, but I have seen enough of the inner workings to think I know which way things are going. I'd like to publish a political prophesy which will be forgotten if it is wrong, but which I can dig out and brag about if it turns out to be right.

The Democrats have demonstrated their ability to throw away presidential elections 4 out of the last 5 times, and they are well on their way to doing it again. My evidence is the huge turnout for the Texas Republican Primary. Whether they were turncoat Democrats or new Republicans doesn't matter, because there were almost twice as many...bad news for Texas Democrats.

I believe the Democrats have sold their souls to so many special interest minorities they can't even remember who they owe what and could never satisfy all the conflicting interests anyway. I believe with just a little economic and international good luck, the voters will throw them out in wholesale lots.

After losing 5 out of 6, the Democrats will no longer be taken seriously in national elections, leaving the Republicans as the dominant national party.

Now that the Republican Party is the most likely way to get into public office, the conflicts between the ultra-conservatives and moderates will become more serious and more damaging to the party.

The conservatives have their own special interest groups. Those who want to force their moral and religious practices on others and their aversion to gambling, drugs, alcohol and sex. Others are so passionately afraid of communism that they would deny political freedom to people in other nations even if they must be killed in order to be saved. Others think the taxpayers should buy agricultural products, music and art work, research and local projects that the users are not willing to pay for.

Others want to support schools in order to control what is being taught to children.

Businessmen are asking the government to grant and enforce monopolies and prevent taxpayers from buying cheaper and better foreign products.

So the Republicans have their own horde of special interest groups all asking for favors at the expense of the taxpayers.

For too long the voters who want less government, lower taxes, and more freedom have been given only a choice of two evils...that is which group of special interest groups to support with their taxes. They should have a third choice, which is NEITHER.

During my lifetime Texas has gone from a one-party state of conservative Democrats where the votes were cast for the man rather than the party, to a two-party state where the choice is between two extremes.

We can't go back, because the old conservative Democratic party no longer exists. Those of us who want low taxes and only the bare minimum government must either form a new moderate party or kick the special interest groups out of the Republican party.

The special interests won't get out voluntarily, so the dominant Republican party will have to split, with the moderates probably taking a new name.

The change will take some time, but the turn of the century will see Texas as a three-party state with the new minimum government party having to work hard to get the voters to the polls whenever their share drops below fifty one per cent.

They will have to be always on guard against people wanting to push special interest legislation through their dominant party.

The best way to protect their purity will be to introduce almost nothing but bills to repeal laws and to vote against almost everything.

The Space Mission—Solar Power Satellite

Ever since I heard Alan Shepherd's radio broadcast from the Mercury capsule, I have been an enthusiastic supporter of the space program. I was keenly interested in the video pictures sent back on Christmas day from the moon and on the subsequent manned landing on the moon. I felt at least a little bit personally involved because one of my closest friends from Texas A&M, Hubert Davis, was the government's chief engineer on the lunar excursion module that safely carried Neil Armstrong and Buzz Aldrin to the surface of the moon and back.

I was also pleased with the 24 successful flights of the space shuttle and just a little bit surprised, but not concerned, when NASA started taking along congressmen and school teachers on orbital flights. When the Challenger blew up in January, 1986, I was shocked and sad, but not surprised. I had known all along that every flight was dangerous. I have been flying my own airplane since 1944 and I know how much more complex the space shuttle is than the puddle jumpers that I am accustomed to flying. There are so many more things that can go wrong.

I assumed that the astronauts and all of the bureaucrats in NASA were also aware of the dangers in every flight and would quickly recover and get the show back on the road with a heightened public awareness of the program and a new respect for the courage of the astronauts who stake their lives on each flight.

The public reaction was just about what I expected. A little bit of investigation and casting around for someone to take the blame for the mistakes, but generally an acceptance of the danger and a determination to move ahead with the program.

The reaction from NASA changed from a casual business as usual attitude toward every flight to a determination to eliminate all risks. Many space engineers were quick to point out that they had been predicting disaster for years and enthusiastically started redesigning the shuttle, eliminating problems that had not yet occurred, making the equipment heavier, delaying the program, and reducing the payload.

Two and half years later, the same process continues with no real hope of getting the program back in operation in 1988. Since the disaster, 23,000 government employees have continued to draw their paychecks at taxpayers' expense and write reports to determine who takes the blame.

There is no need to assign blame for anything. Years ago the shuttle system was predicted to be about 95 per cent perfect. Twenty-four successful flights and one failure works out to be 96 per cent, right on target. What is needed is entirely new leadership for NASA and a new statement of NASA's mission that the taxpayers can understand and accept.

The mission first needs to be determined. Then it will be easier to select the proper leadership. Communications and navigation satellites are already providing benefits to all mankind. The navigation satellites are making ocean and air transportation quicker and safer, but the dollar value of their presence is hard to measure. Communication satellites, however, are being cheerfully paid for by the telephone, television, and data communications companies, who can provide better services to people on earth at lower costs than were previously possible.

Nearly all of the proposed future missions for the space program are of nebulous value. Manufacturing in zero gravity high-vacuum conditions has possibilities, but of unknown worth at this time. Astronomy and exploration of Mars and other parts of the solar system are of scientific value, but it is hard to put a dollar amount on it. Oxygen, aluminum, and silicon can be produced from mines on the moon, but their worth depends on the value of the other space programs which they might support.

The largest space program ever proposed, larger even than the manned mission to Mars, is the one exception. That is the Solar Power Satellite, a ring of monstrous geo-stationary satellites collecting electric power from the sun and beaming it to the Earth by microwave. It could provide enough electricity for all mankind as far into the future as we can foresee. The Solar Power Satellites would dramatically reduce our need for oil, gas and coal. They would eliminate the waste gasses and smoke released from coal-burning electric generating plants, reduce the amount of carbon dioxide released into the atmosphere along with other more harmful gasses, and dramatically reduce the amount of waste heat released into the atmosphere. They would produce an everlasting source of clean, non-polluting electric power.

The cost of such a system is staggering, probably more than a hundred billion dollars, but it is also necessarily an international project. The satellites would be so easy to destroy that they would require treaties and cooperation between nations to be feasible at all. And despite the cost, it would be only a small fraction of the money that is currently being spent on weapons we must never use.

Forty years of mutually assured destruction is enough for anybody. Surely now is the time to begin beating our swords into plowshares and this is a project which the nations of the earth can agree upon.

Since the satellites must be in an equatorial orbit, there is about a 5 per cent saving in fuel if the rockets can be launched from the equator. I propose that a large launching site be established in the Amazon Valley on the equator and fronting on the Atlantic Ocean. In this area hundreds of thousands of engineers and technicians from all over the world would work together assembling and launching the components necessary to build the Solar Power Satellites.

Since the equatorial climate is far from comfortable, the workers should be rotated after no more than three years. In the years it will take to get the system operational, the resident crew would have been exposed to the experience of intense international cooperation. Millions of people would have made new friends in foreign countries and hundreds of thousands would have married foreigners.

We should pursue this project with all the fervency and intensity of a wartime effort. This would be an effort to save mankind from nuclear destruction and to provide mankind with an everlasting source of electric power. Nothing we are doing at this time can be more important than this project. There is no question that it can be made to work. There are serious questions about what it will cost, but if it can be done with money and resources that would otherwise go into totally wasteful weapons, the cost is really of no consequence and the benefits are beyond calculation, but certainly immense.

Legalizing Drugs

Although I don't plan to vote for him, I think Jesse Jackson is the most interesting candidate in the presidential campaign. On at least a few issues he has done some clear thinking and boiled his ideas down into a very few words of memorable poetry.

So far I can't match his style, but maybe with practice I will improve...like playing the piano.

The first idea that comes to mind is an old riddle, "What is the difference between UNLAWFUL and ILLEGAL?" The answer is obvious. "An ill eagle is a sick bird."

TRYING TO STOP THE USE OF UNLAWFUL DRUGS IS MAKING THE AMERICAN EAGLE A SICK BIRD.

I know that's not up to Jessie's standard, but I'll keep working on it.

Chris Mealy, Georgetown's man on the Parole Board, told the Rotary Club that 80 per cent of the people going to jail are hooked on drugs and turned to crime to support their expensive habit.

An old engineer in Houston told me long ago that he was looking for something he could buy for a dime and sell for a dollar that was habit forming. That's the deal on drugs, and if you get caught once in a while, you just spend a little time eating, sleeping, and watching TV at taxpayers' expense. If you behave, Chris Mealy's crew will turn you loose pretty soon to make room for one of your customers who had to steal a TV set to pay for a fix.

We have already been asked to pay taxes for a bond issue to build a bigger jail here. The governor plans to ask for more to expand the Texas prisons.

There are at least two million drug-dependent people in the U.S.A. supporting a 60 BILLION dollar illegal industry. Georgia sheriffs have been offered $100,000 for each drug plane they let land. Corruption cases involving U.S. officers now total 100 per year and are climbing.

We have lost the war on drugs, just like we lost the war on alcohol. Although practicing politicians won't admit it, legalizing drugs is now the only rational option.

More than ten years ago the British Government started selling small quantities of drugs to addicts at low prices. They reported about 2,000 addicts buying the drugs, and no drug-related crime.

Some people have called the "British Experiment" a failure because they did not stop the use of drugs. That's true, but the dope-heads don't have to bother anyone else to get high, and they ARE doing it to themselves.

Sure, it's a waste and a sin, but it doesn't have to be a crime.

The problem isn't the drugs...it's the fact that they are unlawful, and the ILL EAGLE is expensive.

An Encounter Between Spirits

Somewhere, perhaps within the Milky Way Galaxy, and perhaps very far beyond, two spirits met. These encounters don't happen frequently because of the vast size of the universe. As you know, spirits, not being confined by any bodily limitations, are able to travel anywhere they wish at the speed of thought.

There are lots of spirits, many, many billions at least, but they are always busy, doing the things that spirits do, finding planets and other sites suitable for various forms of life, experimenting with farming, breeding, evolution and organizations.

Again, because spirits without bodies have no need for air, water, food, shelter, etc., they are not dependent on each other like we are, but they do like to get together once in awhile to shoot the bull and take advantage of the experience gained by other spirits, just like we do. They do it faster, because they don't suffer from our language problems, and they don't get upset when they learn something new.

Time doesn't mean much to them personally, of course, but the experimental plots they are watching are very much time dependent. Particularly when new mutations of genes and new social experiments are first introduced, the plots need just the right amount of energy, fluids, nutrients and cultivation at just the right time, or they are likely to fizzle without ever being tried. So a spirit needs to watch his experimental plots pretty closely, and just take "time" for a bull session when he has something to report or needs to ask a question.

They don't use names, because there are so many of them, but they recognize each other instantly by their genetic data strings, which they can read at a glance. Since I can't read the data, I'll call them Willie and Joe.

Joe is saying, "Hey, Willie, I heard you had decided to spend a lifetime on that little planet with the Garden of Eden and all the wars. How did it go?"

Willie replies, "I'm a little embarrassed to tell you, but I don't have much to report."

Joe is amazed, "How can that be? You spend a whole life time in one of the most turbulent places in the universe without learning anything useful. You must have had a tragic, early death."

Willie shakes his (head), smiling, "No. As a matter of fact I didn't, and that was the whole problem. As soon as I was locked in I realized I had chosen a poor entry point. The sperm was defective, and the egg came from the same guy's daughter, and the combination was about as bad as it could possibly be."

Joe is sympathetic. "Too bad, but I suppose you miscarried and started over without losing too much time."

"No, the girl's mother was dedicated to one of the religious groups and got the girl the best prenatal care, so I was locked in for another seven months. I had my second chance to escape when I was born, but again my grandmother saw to it that I survived almost a year of surgery and incubators with no chance for me to learn anything except medical technology. I might have gotten away if the grandmother had had to pay for the medical care, but I was covered by an insurance policy."

Joe says, "Well, once you got past the incubator phase you could start picking up useful information."

Willie is still embarrassed. "I might have, but my brain and nervous system were such a mess that I never learned to DO anything. I could see and hear, but I could only eat, drink, shit, and barely move. They put me in a nursing home in Austin for the severely retarded, and I spent my time curled up in a baby bed. Once in a while I happened to be able to see some of the world outside of the nursing home on an electronic thing they call television, but most of the time I was isolated, because they didn't know that I was aware of anything. When anybody came to see me they were so distressed by my appearance that they hardly talked at all."

Joe is really shocked now. "What a miserable trip! I got more out of my tour as a galley slave in the Greek navy. How did you finally get away?"

Willie smiles. "Just a fluke. Some of the people who work in those places are not much brighter than the patients. One of them picked up some gasoline in place of floor polish and blew up one whole wing of the place. The owner was sued for a hundred million dollars by the families of the victims, but we have a big reunion every thousand years to celebrate and honor the housekeeper who got us out of there. Thank God for housekeepers."

Wetbacks Should Be Legal Immigrants

On two beautiful days in January while I was campaigning for the Republican nomination for the U.S. Senate I flew in a light plane from Georgetown to McAllen and then to Houston. From that viewpoint it is not easy to maintain the illusion that Texas is crowded. The population density of Texas is on the order of 50 or 60 people per square mile, roughly comparable to Brazil. Our northeastern states are more than ten times as crowded.

The people who worry about illegal immigrants taking jobs away from natives and sending their children to school at the expense of native taxpayers are focused on the wrong problem.

The problem is not the immigrants, but the fact that they are illegal.

For many years wetbacks have done the least desirable jobs in Texas for less than minimum wages. Because they were illegal, they had essentially no rights. A farmer could work them for two weeks and call the immigration service to send them back to Mexico the day before pay day.

The new law making it illegal for citizens to employ wetbacks has caused more trouble on both sides of the border. Many low-paying jobs are going unfilled, some crops are spoiled, and inflation is ruining many Mexican citizens.

The solution is to make the immigrants legal. I propose that employers operate co-op employment agencies in the border towns. Mexican citizens seeking jobs could cross the border on temporary visas, possibly escorted by immigration officials. Those who found jobs would be picked up by their employers, and the others would be bussed back to Mexico.

Those with jobs would be issued work permits immediately, and would be paid minimum wages or more. These now legal workers would then buy groceries, rent apartments, get driver's licenses, buy used cars and gasoline, pay social security and income taxes. They could live in apartments that might otherwise be vacant. The apartment owners would have more cash to pay school taxes.

Texas would be growing and prosperous. The Texans who are here now would be well advised to buy land at today's prices, because as soon as the immigrants acquire citizenship they will want to buy land.

As usual, the answer is not more laws but the repeal of bad laws.

The people who come to Texas under such a system would be ambitious, and would be willing to pay for lessons in English. Texas could use a million new citizens like these.

The idea that they would be taking jobs away from natives is a short-sighted view. In every town with a growing population, there are more jobs created. A few years ago thousands of people were moving to Houston every day, and Houston was booming. People make jobs for each other.

Ridding Big Corporations Of Bad Management

The Reagan Administration has made one fairly serious miscalculation. They assumed that if corporate taxes were reduced, that businessmen would spend the extra money on modern tools and new products to improve their competitive position.

Instead, many corporations used the excess cash they saved from tax reductions to buy out their competition. This is a much quicker and more certain way to increase profits. New plants and tools are expensive and require many years to pay off and new products are always a big gamble, but buying out your competition will pay off next year for sure.

From a national viewpoint, buying out the competition actually reduces the number of jobs available. Analysts have long known that the Fortune 500 as a group have never produced any new jobs.

Without new tools and new products, corporations lose their competitive edge and begin to suffer from foreign competition. Then they want the government to raise import taxes to protect them from what they call unfair competition.

Big business needs cleaning out periodically. The corporate raiders who have gotten such a bad name in the last few years are just about the only way to get rid of bad management in big corporations.

After many years of success, most big corporations begin to get fat and lazy. They accumulate assets faster than they increase earnings until they reach a point where they are no longer a good investment for their stockholders.

A corporate raider like Boone Pickens looks for a corporation whose stock price is so low because of low earnings that the total market value of all the stock is less than the liquidated value of the assets. In a so-called hostile take-over the raider starts buying the stock at slightly above the market value. When he has enough stock to elect a new board of directors, he fires the management, sells the non-productive assets for enough to pay off his investment, and sells or operates the remainder for a profit.

The stockholders are the winners in such an operation. But the executives of these lazy target corporations are asking for new laws to protect their jobs. The proposed laws are of no benefit to the stockholders and no benefit to the general public. They will only benefit corporate managers who have long needed to be fired.

Water—But Not A Drop To Drink

For the last few years a lot of my brainstorms have been directed to electric generating plants. They were one of the subjects I studied almost forty years ago at Texas A & M, and Eddie Watson, vice president of T U Electric told me last month that the answers to the questions on the exams have not changed much in forty years.

Lately I have been trying to get some of these utility big wigs interested in taking over the development of the Solar Power Satellite system from NASA. So far only Dave Freeman of LCRA has indicated a willingness to go along, but I am still trying.

However there is another problem for electric utility companies that is certainly more 'down to earth,' and that is WATER. Even coal and nuclear plants use tremendous amounts of water to cool and condense the steam before it goes back into the boilers to be reused. The cooling water does not have to be particularly clean, but it does need to be reasonably cool. This water is also recycled, but every time it goes through the plant it gets warm again, and every time it is cooled some of it is lost by evaporation.

At first glance this doesn't seem like any big deal, but it is. When we were talking to the City of Austin engineers about a new power plant south of Georgetown, they said they would need an eighteen inch pipe from Lake Travis just to bring in make-up water. I believe that size pipe would supply all of Georgetown.

Now let's change the subject. In addition to electricity and water, city people need some place to send their water when they are through using it. To keep up with an expanding population we have to keep building waste water treatment plants, and every waste water treatment plant has to have a permit to discharge its 'clean' water into some creek or river.

I have known a little about this subject ever since I helped to build a sewage treatment plant near Paris, Texas for the Army in 1942.

Ordinarily the outflow from a good waste water treatment plant is good enough to drink, but that is true only if the plant is not overloaded. The problem is that the taxpayers seldom want to pay for new plants until the existing plants are overloaded. So the people downstream are somewhat justified in objecting to the discharge permits, because they know that some time in the future the new plant will be old and overloaded, and then it will start dumping slightly dirty water into the creek.

Now we can put two problems together and see if they can make each other disappear.

It turns out that the treated waste water produced by 10,000 people is roughly equal to the evaporation of cooling water needed to produce the electricity for 10,000 people. It also turns out that the make-up water for a power plant does not have to be clean enough to drink.

All we have to do is to combine our waste water treatment plants with our electric generating plants. Then we don't have to steal water from our rivers and we don't have to put dirty water into them. How can you beat a deal like that?

Why don't we get to work on it?

Do We Need An Air Force?

The Battle of Britain started when I was ten years old. The Spitfire and Hurricane pilots were young warriors every bit as glamourous to me as the knights of the round table. That was also a good time to review the exploits of the Newport and Spad pilots of the previous generation. What a thrill for a boy. Four years later I was a pilot myself.

Fortunately I was bitterly disappointed to be left out of the Battle of Midway and the Normandy Invasion. Now I realize that it's only the lucky ones who get old.

I joined the ROTC as soon as I could, but before I could specialize the Army Air Corps had become the U.S. Air Force, and the tactical officers at A & M had started wearing blue suits. I also learned that I would never be an Air Force pilot, because I was slightly near sighted and color blind. But I stuck with it and did well enough to win a free trip to Korea.

I will have to give the interceptor squadrons credit for keeping the MiG's out of our sky. We had many air raid practices, but the only real air raid I had to survive was one night near Seoul when 'Bed Check Charlie' came over in an old biplane and dropped a few hand grenades on us with no damage. Most of the people in my barracks slept thru the raid. Big deal.

Then I learned that the F-84 group that I was supporting near Taegu was not being very effective in helping the infantry. They could only stay up a little over an hour, and at 400 knots they couldn't see much on the ground. They couldn't land with their bombs, so they had to dump them somewhere before they came home, usually on an ox cart.

The close support operation was really an eye opener. An infantry officer could not be trusted to direct the work of an Air Force pilot, so when he needed help he called on an Air Force officer in a jeep, called a forward observer. The forward observer would call in a Cessna Bird Dog or a T-6 trainer and tell him by radio where the target was. The the light airplane would shoot a smoke rocket at the target. If all went well, an F-84 would be flying over and send a high explosive rocket or bomb into the puff of smoke before it drifted too far from the target.

What I heard from my friends in the infantry was that the Marine pilots flying World War II Corsairs were the only ones who could hit anything on the ground.

I asked a fighter/bomber pilot why they didn't attack at 200 knots rather than at 500 knots so they would have more time to aim and not have to pull out of their dive so high. The answer was, "You've got to give us a chance."

After the Korean war the Army essentially gave up on the Air Force for close support and started using their own airplanes and helicopters. The last time I heard the Army had a bigger air force than THE Air Force. Of course the Navy does the same.

So what mission does that leave for the Air Force? The air interceptor role has essentially vanished, because the Soviets don't have an impressive bomber force for us to intercept. That leaves strategic bombing.

Quoting from Fred Reed, military columnist for Universal Press Syndicate, "Except in strange and contrived scenarios, by the time the bombers reach the Soviet Union, the ICBMs will already have arrived, and the bombers will have nothing to do but rearrange the rubble."

One argument is that bombers can be called back, which appeals to people who think the next war might start by accident, but when the first missile explodes here, our submarines will launch their missiles.

Others say that the bombers can be kept aloft and armed 24 hours per day, but still the submarines will beat them to the punch.

Argument three says a radar invisible bomber can penetrate Soviet airspace and wipe out their missiles BEFORE the general nuclear exchange. We would have to start the war.

Argument four says the war might not be over after we swap ICBMs, and the bombers can pound the Soviets into submission.

Argument five says we can force the Soviets to divert money into air defense. That makes the bombers an economic weapon that may cost us more than it costs them.

Argument six says the bombers are proven, and the missiles might not work.

Again quoting Reed, "In sum, the bombers will attack before the main war, or after it in a drawn-out grudge match, or bomb a Soviet Union already wrecked by missiles, or spend the Soviets to death. Alternatively, we need bombers because we're not sure our missiles will even work. There is a quality of trying too hard in all of this."

"Both the Navy and the Marine Corps have their own fighters and use them well. Minuteman missiles could be considered artillery and could easily come under Army control. Loss of the bombers would take the Air Force one step closer to being divided up."

That would take us back to what worked fairly well in the last 'popular war' and would cost the taxpayers a lot less than the present system.

Time To Move On To The Stars

Neil Armstrong and his supporters at NASA made me proud to be and American and an engineer when they landed on the Moon almost 20 years ago.

When I watched the Challenger blow up on TV just two years ago I was stunned but not surprised. I hoped the disaster would not set the American space program back too far.

But it has. At this point I am ashamed of our leadership. They have acted as if the American people will insist on absolute safety and will withdraw support for any risky project.

At the time of the disaster, there had been 24 successful shuttle flights, and the Challenger itself had flown several times without trouble. The cause of the wreck was determined just a few weeks later, and flights could have been resumed immediately with the remaining spacecraft.

There would have been no shortage of volunteer pilots and crews. I have flown more than 3,000 hours since 1944, and I have always known that every flight carried some risk. Every American astronaut since Alan Sheppard has freely accepted the risk of death on every flight, and for this reason they are legitimate heroes.

But their bosses are not. 23,000 bureaucrats are afraid that some investigator will find them responsible for a fatal mistake, and they might lose THEIR JOB.

Now the Soviets have a right to be proud of their space program and to look down on the "gutless Americans."

I want to change this situation.

First—I believe we should immediately resume shuttle flights.

Second—I believe we should immediately begin building a permanent manned station in low earth orbit. This will facilitate further exploration of the Solar system and the building of a SOLAR POWER SATELLITE.

Third—I believe we should offer to cooperate with the Soviets in building the manned space station. We can probably learn about as much as we can teach on this project.

Fourth—We should set our NASA engineers to work studying the missiles that are scheduled to be scrapped to determine how they can best be converted to peaceful freighters.

Fifth—I believe we should take advantage of the coming nuclear missile treaty to convert missiles into freight carriers. Each missile should be able to carry a ton or more of valuable payload into orbit, and the empty fuel tanks will also be of value.

We have had enough of "Mutually Assured Destruction."

It is time to "BEAT OUR SWORDS INTO PLOWSHARES" and move on to the stars.

Money Should Be Crystallized Sweat

There are at least a dozen people who read this column regularly, and they know about Willie and Joe, but a short introduction will be helpful to those who are with us for the first time.

Willie and Joe are two of billions of spirits who have existed forever and who travel at will all over the universe cultivating new biological forms and social systems wherever they find suitable environments. Once every thousand years or so, two of them will get together to compare their experiences. We are eavesdropping on one of their bull sessions.

Willie is saying, “I have lived several times now on that little planet with the Garden of Eden and all the wars, and they do come up with some cute ideas. Have you ever heard of MONEY?”

Joe is at a total loss.

“Well, it’s a sophisticated way of increasing prosperity by letting individuals do what they do best and trading their labor with others who specialize in different things.”

Joe says, “Oh yeah, that’s what we did on my Neanderthal tour. The women were seldom able to go hunting, because they were always pregnant or nursing. Most of the babies weren’t fit or lucky enough to grow up, so we had to have lots of them. I had to get in on five conceptions before I ever got big enough to hunt. Plenty of excitement after that, though. You wouldn’t believe some of the game we tackled, working together. The gals kept the fires going, made the clothes, dried the meat, raised the kids and generally made life worth living.”

Willie agrees, “That’s the basic idea, but in my tribe we had a guy who had lost a leg who got to be an expert at making arrowheads. He would trade three beautiful little flint tips for a dead rabbit, and he ate better than most of the hunters. He taught me how to make them, and I was able to travel hundreds of miles without taking time to hunt. The small ones were worth more than the big ones, because they took more time to produce, so I could travel light. Everywhere I stopped I could trade for food, clothes, shoes, and everything I needed."

Joe is impressed. "Say, we could use that in the Andromeda Galaxy except that nobody hunts there. They are all vegetarians."

Willie has the answer. "We didn't stick with arrowheads forever. Several thousand years later I lived with a bigger bunch that used gold. We could travel even lighter, because gold is never found in large quantities. It takes a hundred times more work to round up an ounce than it takes to make an ounce of arrowheads. It just takes a few thousand years to get general agreement that an ounce of gold is worth a month of food and lodging."

Joe is really fired up now. "I see. Money is just crystallized sweat. Say, we've got something like that gold stuff. I can't wait to give it a try."

But Willie is cautious. "There is still a problem. Later on we got carried away with travelling light and invented paper certificates and credit cards worth a hundred ounces of gold."

Suddenly Joe is concerned. "How do you keep people who haven't made any arrowheads from printing papers that say they have?"

Willie sighs, "Well, the government makes that a crime. The only trouble is that there is nobody to keep the government from giving away pieces of paper that nobody did any work for."

Joe is amazed. "Why would they do that?"

"To buy votes. I guess it's better than the old system of kings."

Joe is disappointed. "Sounds like you need an honest government."

Willie agrees. "Yeah, we're working on that."

Another Political Prophesy
Swords Into Plowshares
September 24, 1988

I do some of my most creative work after five when the office gets quiet. However, once or twice a month the world's greatest conversationalist drops in for a visit about six.

I put up with this guy because he is always enthusiastic, he listens to what I say with GREAT interest, and he tells me what has been on TV, saving me untold hours in front of the boob tube.

He told me the presidential campaign was just about a toss-up, and that he had decided to vote for Bush for President and Bentsen for Senator, which would probably be good for Texas if what we can expect is politics as usual.

This prompted me to go public with my next GREAT SNEAD POLITICAL PROPHESY:

For better or worse, Bush has it in the bag. Remember, Reagan came home from Moscow last May all smiles, but without any agreement. I believe he and Gorbachev have settled on a real sweetheart deal they are saving to announce at a dramatic time, the anniversary of the October revolution in Russia, and just before election time here. George Bush will hammer out the final details and bring in the signed contract.

I will go even farther out on a limb and guess that the deal will be a U.S./Soviet joint venture manned expedition to Mars.

Something like this is almost essential if peace breaks out next year. Without a constant threat from our traditional evil enemy, millions of Americans who design and build the tools of destruction could be out of a job, and we would have a real 1930-style depression on our hands. Fortunately the same skills and tools needed for radar proof bombers and laser tank gun sights will work just as well for building space craft.

I will be delighted with the prospect of peace, but a little disappointed if they don't think of something more useful. My favorite monster project is the Solar Power Satellite, which would make electricity from sunlight and send it to earth by a harmless microwave beam. In one generation this would begin to clean up our air and water, reduce our dependence on foreign oil and provide every one of eight billion people with a fifty horsepower electrical slave.

My consolation is that both the TRIP TO MARS and the SOLAR POWER SATELLITES will need a mining base on the moon to provide cheap oxygen, aluminum and silicon. Our electric generating utilities will get a free ride for the first ten years. The taxpayers will buy the heavy lift launch vehicles (hydrogen powered, I hope) and the Lunar Oxygen and Metals plant and thereby eliminate almost all the risk when the electric utilities decide to move ahead.

Incidentally, there is no need to worry about either the fantastic cost or adequate national defense. None of this will happen fast. We can make very small, cautious reductions in the defense budget, apply part of the savings to the national debt, another part to social programs, and still have more than enough for the big space venture.

We can carefully watch the Soviets make similar reductions in war materials, provide more consumer goods for their people, and expect them to show up at the launch site with their part of the space materials and technicians.

Incidentally, this prophesy is not entirely new. About 2,800 years ago a guy named Micah said, "They will beat their swords into plowshares and their spears into pruning hooks; nations shall no longer fight each other, for all war will end."

The way things are going we just might make it in time for Jesus' two thousandth birthday. I think He would be pleased.

24 September 1988

To: Lake Buchanan State Bank
P. O. Box 468
Buchanan Dam, Texas 78609

Pay to the order of George Bush for President Campaign $1,000.00 One Thousand Dollars Only on condition that he endorse this check personally and certify that he has read my Ex-Candidate's Report Number Thirteen, dated 24 September 1988.

____

Edwin DeS. Snead
1400 Vine Street
Georgetown, Texas 78626

Account Number: 0309 0400 0378

Deposit for ______________________________________

I certify that I have read Mr. Snead's Ex-Candidate's Report Number 13.

__________________________ __________________

George Bush Date

The "American Economic Community"

Forty years ago the world was one big market for everything, and the U.S.A. was the only undamaged industrial nation ready to supply the goods.

Now nearly everybody has plenty to sell and is ready to work for lower wages and sell cheaper than we are.

This situation is not going to get any better for us.

In less than four years all of the trade barriers in Europe are scheduled to be eliminated, but only for members, and we have not been invited to join. It is much more likely that Europeans will feel a need to protect their growing industries from American competition.

By the word "America" we generally mean the United States of America, and this national myopia keeps us from seeing the world's greatest opportunity.

There are more Americans who speak Spanish and Portuguese than there are who speak English. All together we Americans are more numerous than Europeans, and we have more living room and more natural resources waiting to be developed.

America is still the New World and the land of opportunity. It is our natural sphere of influence, easily connected by roads and railroads, all basically in one time zone, and surrounded by a navigable moat three thousand miles wide and several miles deep.

There is probably enough petroleum for all America's immediate needs in the U.S., Mexico and Venezuela, although at a higher price than oil from the Persian Gulf. But, while we buy oil from the cheapest source, we plan to let our taxpayers bail out banks who cannot collect on loans from oil producing American nations.

We need an American Economic Community now, and we will need it much more in just a few years.

These hundreds of millions of "Other Americans" are eager to trade with us and share in our prosperity, but they are stymied by one big problem, our amazing self-righteousness. There are only two ways to do anything, our way and the wrong way.

The most immediate problem is our attitude toward drugs. We insist on making criminals out of people who are stupid, weak, or sick, and then on making war on the simple farmers and smugglers who respond to the fantastic demand and fantastic prices we create by our fantastic efforts to stop people from harming themselves.

No matter how badly we need an American Economic Community, we can not even begin to create it until we abandon the idea that all our friends must share our fantasies.

Turning Sunlight Into Electricity

I applied for my first patent almost twenty years ago and have been issued one almost every year since. I have learned two very important things about being an inventor:

First, the secret of success is to start rich and work your way down.

Second, it is much easier to make an idea work than it is to sell it to the public.

When I ran for the Senate, it was not because I wanted the job, but because I was appalled by the silliness and insanity I had seen in government. I thought the government and the public would welcome some new ideas. I should have known better.

A politician cannot be a leader until he has been in government long enough to be unbeatable in the next election. By then he has fought enough election campaigns and watched enough colleagues come and go, so that he knows as much about the election business as I know about the invention business. Here is the first rule of elections:

If you want to be a leader, find a parade and get in front of it.

The big problem is to find the parade before the election. They used to say, "Run it up the flagpole and see if anybody salutes." But a politician cannot afford to be identified with something until he is pretty sure the public is behind it. Otherwise he is likely to be identified as a dangerous, visionary crackpot, or worse yet, ignored.

Computers and statistics have come to the rescue in the form of polls. By carefully selecting a representative sample of the general public, pollsters claim to be able to measure the attitudes of many millions of people by asking only a few thousand.

Chief executives of big corporations are not quite as sensitive to public opinion as politicians are, but they depend on their customers to vote with their checkbooks when they buy the corporation's products or its stock. The results are not as sudden as an election, but it's just as sure. Don't irritate the customers...your job depends on them.

What am I leading up to? I'm glad you asked. Thanks for reading this far.

I know about a very large project which has not become popular yet, but it must, and its time is now.

It is the best, and in some cases the only answer to all of these well-known problems:

Depletion of oil and gas reserves
The foreign trade imbalance
Air pollution and acid rain
Carbon dioxide and the greenhouse effect
The ozone hole over Antarctica
Disposal of spent nuclear fuel
Three Mile Island and Chernobyl fears
Possible wars over foreign oil
Electrical brownouts
Energy needs in developing countries
An economic reason for space exploration
A long-term solution to population pressure
The threat of nuclear war

These are all popular problems without popular solutions, but there is a solution to all of them that deserves further study...the Solar Power Satellite project.

Twenty years ago Dr. Peter Glaser proposed a ring of monstrous satellites in geo-stationary orbit, turning sunlight into electricity 24 hours a day and sending it to earth by harmless microwave beams.

At the time most engineers, including myself, considered the project ridiculous, but ten years ago NASA spent sixteen million dollars looking for the fatal flaw and could not find one. They concluded that it would work with technology existing at that time, but it would cost more than they thought the taxpayers would pay. But they also pointed out that in the 25 years it would take to build it, the electric utilities would have to spend about eight times as much on coal and nuclear plants to satisfy the demand for electricity, adding to some of the problems listed above.

What I propose is to let the electric utilities take over the project for three reasons:

They will eventually have to sell the electricity.
They will have to spend the money anyway.
They can do it cheaper than any government agency.

But of course, like the government, the only money the utilities have to spend must come from their customers. Every taxpayer is also an electric customer, so what's the difference?

A big difference....

The project would not have to be resold to the public every election year (lower cost).

The money would not have to be spent in ways that would help to re-elect Congressmen (lower costs).

Every launch would not have to be a big public relations event with Congressmen and school teachers aboard. Most flights would be unmanned (lower costs).

Flight safety would be less important, allowing larger payloads and lower costs.

Electric customer could vote on this one project instead of the dozens of issues in a political election.

The big question right now is, "Would the electric customers support the project?" I say, "Let's ask them."

Every month the electric utilities send out millions of bills, and customers send back their checks. The postage is already being paid. For just the cost of printing, we could describe the project and ask the customers if they would be willing to pay about two cents a month for a couple of years to bring the research on the Solar Power Satellite up to date, and then a gradual increase to about two dollars a month as long as the project is making progress.

The results of such a survey, even in one city, would be more convincing than a political poll.

The utility executive who takes the first poll like this would be taking only a very small risk, and would have a graceful way out if the results were negative.

If the results were positive, it would be the start of a parade that anyone could safely step in front of.

Like the Marines, all we need now are a few good men.

The Whale Tale And Christmas
December 11, 1988

Last week I was in New York City for a board meeting of a small company. Mikhail Gorbachev was in town the day before, but because of the earthquake in Armenia he had to leave so suddenly that he did not have time to leave a message at my hotel.

Then on the flight back to Texas I glanced at the U.S.A. Today newspaper over the shoulder of another passenger and noticed a headline about aid to the earthquake victims.

If you look hard enough, you can find something good about almost everything, and I began to see a pattern of bad news turning to good news which fits in beautifully with the Christmas season.

When I was campaigning for the Senate last winter I met a lot of good, solid Republicans who sincerely believe that the only good communist is a dead communist. Even if this were a good, safe generality, I suspect that most of them would concede an exception here and there.

Last month when the rescue of the whales was in the news, the climax to the story was the arrival of the Soviet icebreaker. Certainly the skipper and probably most of the crew were good communists, but they deserve at least a little grudging respect for the part they played in the whale tale.

But of course the whale tale was not universally applauded. There were a few old soreheads who felt that the attention and effort devoted to the rescue of the whales would have been better spent on needy humans. It's hard to argue with that point of view.

But lo and behold the very next month along comes an opportunity to help some people, and of all people, the Armenians.

Just a few weeks earlier some of the same people may have been marching in the streets demanding independence from the Soviet Union. Here is a Heaven-sent opportunity for Mikhail Gorbachev and the rest of the Soviet leadership to demonstrate their concern for a small part of their empire.

In the midst of electric power failures, and shortages of food, housing, water and medical help, the arrival of Soviet trucks, trains and airplanes loaded with emergency supplies and personnel will be a welcome sight.

Surely the Soviet Union is big enough and strong enough to provide all the necessary relief for their own earthquake victims, but it could also be an opportunity for the capitalist nations to demonstrate their own concern for human suffering in a tangible way.

This would of course precipitate another outcry from the soreheads. Certainly there are enough needy people within our own borders. And from a cold war viewpoint any kind of trouble within the Soviet Union is bound to be good for our side. If we had been supplying freedom fighters in Armenia, an earthquake would have been an accomplishment beyond their wildest dreams.

Probably we won't even be invited to help, but I believe we should make the offer anyway. This month we celebrate the birthday of an unusual man who told us we should love our enemies. Here is a chance to give it a try and see if it leads to peace on earth and good will toward men.

Let Horses Carry The Colors

Just before Christmas the Fightin' Texas Aggie Football Team was in the news. The most effective head coach in my generation was released from his long term contract amidst suspicions of paying too much to recruit talented students who can incidentally also play football.

The super-aggies in the coffee gang at the L & M Cafe were heartbroken, sick and indignant about such hypocrisy. Since everybody does it, why not make it legal?

In another bull session (us Aggies are good at this) I heard that football is the only reason some boys stay in high school. Without it they might be on the streets selling dope.

College football scholars are competing for the highest paying graduate fellowships that exist in the professional football leagues. A bachelor's degree is not a prerequisite for matriculation in these institutions, but some undergraduate experience is almost essential.

Football, or something like it, is probably essential for building school spirit, getting donations from rich alumni, and keeping lots of kids in school. Playing in the marching band was certainly the most fun I had in high school, and other kids might have dropped out without the girls' pep squad and marching team.

All through my career at Texas A & M, I yelled myself hoarse telling those Fightin' Texas Aggies to BEAT HELL OUTA TEA YOU. That encouragement was almost all for the football team, because we didn't seem to get much satisfaction out of BEATIN' HELL OUTA TEA YOU in tennis or swimming. I must not have put enough spirit in it, because all the time I was there those fightin' Texas Aggies were never able to beat T. U. in football.

Nobody seemed to care that those were not our fellow students we were yelling for. They slept in a dormitory in a different part of the campus and ate in a different mess hall. I can't remember ever having a class with one of the football players. They had a private swimming pool, the only air conditioned dorm on the campus and tutors to help them pass enough courses to stay in school.

But all this was acceptable, because if our school didn't have a good football team, we just "didn't get no respect."

Some time during my senior year I read an essay about college football. The author observed that it was a very expensive and risky undertaking for a college. In order to sell enough tickets to pay for a winning team, you had to build a huge stadium...a multi-million dollar investment to be used only three months a year. Then to get enough people to buy tickets to pay for the stadium, you had to have a winning team. And if one team is winning, the others must be losing. So it's hard for ONE college to make a profit on football, and impossible for ALL colleges.

The author of the essay suggested that we might have just as much fun on a Saturday afternoon at a horse race as we would at a football game. The horses could carry the school colors, the bands could play, the virgins could dance, and Monday morning the horses would not have to be in classes.

So gettin' back to us Aggies. After BEATIN' HELL OUTA TEA YOU five years in a row, we've been banned in Boston and lost the best coach we ever had. What are we gonna do next?

I say it's time to declare victory in the football marathon and move on to something better. Horse racing has just been legalized in Texas, and Texas A & M has the only veterinary school in Texas. The Aggies already have a head start.

We should get the boys in the welding class to build a high-tech starting gate to fit on the track at Kyle Field with enough stalls for every school in the Southwest Conference. The agricultural students could raise mushrooms on the by-products. If the Aggies get into it first, it could be a real money maker.

We'd have a few hundred slightly used gladiator suits which could be used for intramural athletics like they do at Southwestern University. A few of the suits would be small enough to keep the real students from hurting each other.

Move Up Or Out—The Two Term Limit

Several weeks ago banker Charles Parker sent me a copy of Bud Buckner's editorial in the *Llano News* about the huge pay raise for congressmen, cabinet members and federal judges. He thought it would be "a very good topic for an ex-candidate's report."

I thought the proposal might die because of scrutiny by the press, but it hasn't, and it came up in a church sermon today.

When I decided to run for the Senate I didn't know and didn't care what the salary would be. I thought I was on a mission. But as I got into the process it became more and more obvious that the cost of getting elected would be many times any conceivable salary.

If the salaries were little or nothing, then the only the rich could afford to serve in the government. We don't want that, but we need a better deal for the people.

After the primary I spent a few days in Washington. The only hotel room available cost well over two hundred dollars a day. It's a busy town, populated almost entirely by government employees, lawyers and lobbyists trying to get congress and the regulators to give them something at the taxpayers' expense, or trying to keep from getting a big bill for someone else's government handout.

The stakes are so big that it's a mistake not to do everything that's legal to influence those in power. Big fees for speeches and plant tours, and ten thousand dollar breakfasts are not illegal now, so they can't be bribery. It's legal for a trial lawyer to make a $10,000 campaign contribution to a judge who will soon be hearing his case, because judges cannot be influenced by such things. Otherwise they would not be judges.

It's a little hard for us laymen to understand the difference between bribery and the usual cost of doing business, but our congressmen are willing to outlaw some of this in exchange for a pay raise. If we can't get a better deal, we probably should accept the one they've offered.

What sounds like a better deal to me was suggested by Henry B. Fox of Circleville in his book, *Dirty Politics is Fun.*

He proposed that congressmen be limited to two terms in office, just like the president. The president's limit was fixed by a Constitutional amendment not too long ago.

Under such a system no one could rise by seniority to the top of important committees and be more secure in his job than the president. People like this don't need to take bribes. Every lobbyist in town will do anything for them that is legal just for a chance to be heard. We want them to listen. We just hope they listen to lobbyists from both side of every issue.

A two-term limit would not keep some people from being professional politicians, but it would thin the ranks considerably. If, after two terms, a fellow had to move up or out, not too many would make it.

This Man Likes Comfortable Clothes

My mother always wanted me to wear nice clothes and to have an overcoat. She bought me a nice overcoat once or twice when we were going to a rock crushing convention in Chicago or Washington in the winter.

There were a couple of times when the overcoat felt good when I was walking around Chicago in the snow. It was needed just for a few minutes waiting for a taxi, and at other times I had to rent a parking space for it.

I also noticed that all the yankees wearing overcoats were really not dressed very well for winter. Their city shoes did not keep their feet warm or dry, and their necks, ears, chins and noses were cold. Those with bald heads had to have a hat, but with a nice overcoat they looked dignified and prosperous.

When I joined the Air Force in 1951, I received several hundred dollars for a uniform allowance. I bought everything but the overcoat and used the extra money for an engagement ring. As long as I stayed in the States I had a wife to keep me warm, and in Korea we didn't wear the dress blues much anyway.

In some ways the military is practical about clothes. Khaki underwear doesn't show the dirt and doesn't give away your position when it is hanging out to dry. Fatigues have huge pockets that nothing can spill out of. A steel helmet won't stop a bullet, but it's some comfort when anti-aircraft shell fragments are falling out of the sky.

For four years in the R.O.T.C. and two years in the Air Force I never had to make any decisions about clothes. Some one else made all the important decisions for me, about like ny wife does now. Generally the clothes they picked were appropriate for the occasion, but when the military decides to really dress up, they are even sillier than the civilians. Dress uniforms always remind me of the scene from "The Five Thousand Fingers of Dr. T" when Dr. Terwilliger was being draped with gold braid from a reel.

I like to wear lace-up boots with soft arch supports and non-skid soles. With them I never get rocks in my shoes and seldom sprain an ankle on uneven ground.

Blue jeans are comfortable indoors or outdoors in summer or winter. In really cold weather long johns are nice under the blue jeans, but they are a problem indoors. The right thing for winter is a loose fitting jump suit with a hood. A pair of gloves and a wool cap in the outer pockets make it almost the ideal winter garment...far better than an overcoat, and cheaper.

For rainy weather the jump suit should be made of water repellent fabric and it should be yellow to show up on dark days through rain-splattered windshields.

In the summer a long-sleeve cotton shirt will soak up sweat and prevent sunburn. I have trouble with hats, leaving them in restaurants and having them blow away. The only practical hat I have ever seen is the old Stetson beaver. The little string around the band with the button on the end is supposed to be stuck thru a button hole to keep the hat from blowing away. I have never seen anybody wear one that way.

Neckties and rings should be outlawed around machinery. I have never understood why any man needs a necktie at any time. I don't even wear my Aggie ring. I figure if a man is an Aggie he will tell you, and if he's not, there's no point in embarrassing him.

I travel a lot, and I have noticed that the really experienced travellers on transocean flights wear sweat suits and jump suits. Any clothes will look like they have been slept in when you get there anyway. My wife has not let me travel this way yet, and it would be too expensive to replace her.

I keep hoping the modern world will get sensible about clothes. The crew on the starship Enterprise look pretty nice, but of course they are all built like movie actors. The rest of us need something to hide our pot bellies.

In the old days the king set the styles. I don't believe George Bush will be any help along these lines, and Prince Charles doesn't seem like the type either. Until our liberator comes along I'll just have to keep wearing my businessman disguise for ceremonial occasions.

Lick The Garbage Problem

I have unusual friends. On my last trip to New York I visited a garbage dump operated by a new friend.

This one was on Long Island, and it was not a smelly place, although it could easily have been. My friend had started his career as a trucker. He now owns an auto parts store, and a big sand pit where he disposes of waste concrete and other industrial waste for a handsome profit.

This was no shabby operation. He complies strictly with every environmental regulation, sealing off the pits with plastic sheets and compacted clay. He takes the old reinforcing steel out of the concrete and sells the crushed concrete for road material. It made me wish I felt young and eager enough to do something like it in Texas.

Every time someone mentions garbage I think of Louie Welch, who was mayor of Houston when I lived there. He said," Everybody wants you to pick up the garbage, but nobody wants you to put it down." At that time the City of Houston was paying seven dollars a ton to people who could make garbage disappear. That was more than I was getting for crushed stone, and now the going price in a big city is several times that.

There is lots of valuable stuff in garbage, but it's all mixed up in a big dirty mess. Most of the valuable stuff in it is not worth the cost of separating it from all the other stuff.

In the last few years I have been in Kinshasa, Zaire and Bombay, Nagpur and Calcutta, and found that they don't have much of a garbage problem. In the first place, they don't waste as much as we do, but the big difference is that by the time the poor people get through picking it over, there is not enough left to feed the birds and goats. They use every scrap of paper for toilet paper, the cans and unbroken bottles, and the stuff they can't use just turns to sand.

The difference is that our poor people are not as poor as theirs, and there are not enough of them to take care of our garbage problem. Our goats are just like theirs, but we don't let them run loose in the cities.

We have long known that we need to recycle the materials in garbage, but we have not done much about it. It is just not practical to require an aluminum plant or a paper mill or a bottle factory to dispose of garbage. By the time they pay for cleaning it up, it costs more than their regular raw materials. And if they miss something in the cleaning process, they could ruin a big batch of finished product that would cost many times what they might have saved on raw materials.

The answer is to not make garbage in the first place. A bag of clean aluminum cans is not garbage, and neither are clean glass bottles with the brown, green and clear ones all in separate bags. Back during the last popular war we turned in our kitchen grease, tooth paste tubes and tin cans to help the war effort. Materials that are cleaned and separated may be scrap or salvage, but they are not garbage.

Every house needs several different garbage cans, called by a new name, "salvage cans." They could be lined with distinctively marked bags of either plastic or paper, and should have the home owner's address pre-printed on them. The salvage trucks could still pick up the bags on a regular day, but the various materials would be kept separate and hauled to separate recycling plants or collection depots.

Home owners who cooperate with the system could be charged much less for the collection service. They might even get it free or be paid for the materials. Those who insist on mixing everything together and manufacturing garbage would pay a much higher price. They might even have to dispose of the stinky mess themselves, and pay somebody at the "dump" to make it disappear.

We can lick the garbage problem at its source, but it does require that neighbors work together. And it would be easier to start in a small town.

Leave Abortion "Issue" To Qualified Experts

I had a small shock last week. I got a newsletter in the mail from Mike Richards, who like me, is not a candidate for anything, but the publication made it clear that he is available.

I could see immediately how my series of Ex-Candidate's Reports would lead people to believe that I am also still running for some public office. That needs to be cleared up.

In addition to spending a whole lot of my own money and getting a good lesson in humility, I learned that there is no public job available that I want at all...much less enough to campaign for it. I thought it was something I had to do, but the people gave me an honorable discharge, for which I am grateful.

Mike Richards is a capable and charming young man, and would probably make a pretty good public servant. However, about this time last year we were both addressing a group of super conservatives in Houston. I was sitting by Mike's wife while he delivered a passionate speech opposing a woman's right to terminate a pregnancy by abortion. I would have felt more comfortable sitting by Mike while Cynthia delivered the speech. I didn't have enough nerve to ask her if she agreed with her husband.

I suppose it's OK with me if people want to pass some new laws regulating abortions, provided the people who draft the laws and debate their merit are qualified experts on the subject. I propose that every person who takes any part in this issue, including legislators, judges, juries, and legal counsels be required to demonstrate his (or her) ability to conceive and bear children and to furnish them with milk from his (or her) own body.

I wish Mike the best of luck in his next campaign provided he will leave this particular issue to Cynthia.

A Letter To A Young Man

Dear Son,

Congratulations on your accomplishments over the last years in a tough environment... a high rank in the corps, your extracurricular activities, and your better than average grades.

Now I understand that you would like to continue your education at Texas A & M, where I went to school many years ago. I understand that your high school grades are not quite up to the new Aggie standards, and you would like my help in getting into the summer provisional program where 2,000 students are competing for 500 spots.

First, you need to know that the only "influence" I have at A & M is in the Cadet Corps where I have arranged for a few scholarships for Eagle Scouts who want to take advantage of the excellent leadership training available there. I know you have suffered through enough "military bullshit" to last the rest of your life. That puts you in a class with almost every man who has ever worn a uniform, in war or peace.

Even if Peace breaks out, for which I fervently hope, we will still need an Army and Navy composed of our best men and women. I also believe we need Citizens/Soldiers instead of Mercenaries who, when they have finished their military service, can vote intelligently for the real needs of our armed services.

Also please remember that this nation is just loaded with people who make average grades, but who want a diploma from a good university, and a good job that pays well for not too much work in a pleasant environment.

These same people want to pay low taxes and have their money worth more than anybody else's so they can buy automobiles, cameras and computers dirt cheap from people who spent twice as much time in school and who work for half the wages.

I am proud of the fact that I am an engineer, and that most of my career has been spent getting construction materials out of the ground and helping to build cities where millions of ordinary people can live and work in health and comfort.

Only the farmers are doing more to make it possible for lawyers and bookkeepers to spend their lives in air conditioned buildings and cars.

Your father is one the best men I know, and I would do almost anything for him. You are a good kid and have come a long way in the last few years. I will be glad to help you any way I can when I am convinced that you are going to be an outstanding and productive leader.

I plan to let the government take care of the ordinary people.

Sincerely yours,

E. deS. Snead

Opening The Rail System

A Letter to:
Senator Lloyd Bentsen
Senate Office Building
Washington, D.C.

Dear Mr. Bentsen:

First I want to thank you for the part you played in stopping the 50% pay raise for Congressmen.

Next, I want to tell you how pleased I am about the way the 1988 election turned out. The people of Texas and the United States are better off with you in the Senate than they would have been if by some strange turn of events I had won your position. I would not have the patience to do the job you are doing.

When we visited in your office a year ago, I offered to advise you on a bill to effect some re-regulation of the railroads, a field in which I have some firsthand experience.

As I studied the bill, I was repelled by the tedious legal jargon which made the intent and effect difficult to understand. On closer reading, it became apparent that its purpose was to reduce the abuse of one monopoly, the electric utilities, by another monopoly, the railroads, by imposing more government regulation. I doubt that the people would benefit much from it.

Deregulation has been hard on my small railroad for the past few years, but our situation has been improving gradually as we are able to make the big railroads compete for our business.

If any new law is needed, it should do far more than just try to regulate a monopoly. It should be possible to make the entire railway system open to all qualified carriers, like the highway, airway, and waterway systems are now. A system of unlimited running rights and cooperative maintenance-of-way could eliminate the monopolies while keeping the advantages of private ownership.

However, as a general rule, I believe this country does not need more laws as much as it needs to repeal bad laws.

If I were in your office, and I thank God that I am not, I would vote against any new law that was not clearly a WIN/WIN deal for all the hard-working people in the country. That would probably include the bill you asked me to review, along with most of the other bills introduced every year.

Thanks again for a good job. Keep up the good work.

Sincerely yours,

Ned Snead

The World Needs More Love—Not Babies

A healthy man with unlimited opportunities could produce about five thousand sons and daughters.

Fortunately, half of the people in the world are women, and each one of them can only produce about twenty. However, that is still ten times as many babies as we need to stay even.

At the maximum rate, in a few hundred years we could be completely out of elbow room. Actually, the rate would be forced to drop off earlier when we run out of room to lie down.

Even long before that we will run out of food, and the smell will be hard to take, even after you get used to it.

A couple of years ago I spent a few weeks in India. They still have some open space left, except in the cities. The place must have been a paradise for British businessmen...lots of cheap labor to produce the cotton, and a fantastic market for sewing machines and bicycles. The British are gone now, and the Indians are making some progress on the problems the British were too busy to bother with.

We have lots of wide open space in North and South America. We don't have to worry about things getting as bad here as they are in India for a couple of generations. I expect to be dead by then.

Some good people say, "If you don't want babies, don't make love." That would be a sure-fire system, but I believe the world needs love five thousand times as much as it needs babies. If we cut back too far on love, people will get so mean they won't be fit to live with.

For thousands of years many of the world's leaders have thought they needed to breed bumper crops of soldiers, farmers, taxpayers and voters. Even now, when a politician mentions birth control, the opposition accuses him of trying to undercut their base of support. They are right, of course. Without down-trodden masses, where could an ambitious leader find enough followers to get himself elected? But who wants to raise a soldier for that kind of army?

A few years ago families needed lots of kids to work the farm and make up for early deaths. Now it costs a bunch to send a kid to college. Graduates earn more than drop-outs, so a small family is likely to turn out better off financially.

Last week in London a lady doctor told me that a "morning-after" birth control pill is available by prescription in England. I asked her what was in it, and she said, "Just an overdose of estrogen." I have no idea what the side effects might be, but it's something a lady should ask her doctor about if she's not ready for another twenty years of hard labor as a mother.

There are all kinds of other options available, and fortunately I don't need any of them. But I would suggest that the rest of you lovers get smarter.

Women Politicians

Last night the Texas Republican Party gathered to honor Governor Bill Clements, the first Republican Governor of Texas in more than a hundred years.

The highlight of the evening was the presentation of a beautiful Steuben Glass sculpture of the silver sword *Excalibur* and a reference to the miraculous designation of the legendary Arthur as King of England.

However, like most modern miracles, the appearance of businessman Bill Clements as the leader of a bunch of Texas politicians was explained in the same ceremony.

Bill's wife, Rita, was the hardest-working politician in Texas while Bill was rising to prominence in the business world. She had already elected Dwight Eisenhower and John Tower when she finally persuaded Bill to run for office. Her speech last night in her deep, authoritative voice was enough to convince anyone where the real power in Texas politics lies, with the women.

Ruth Fox, president of the Texas Republican Women, arranged the first-class event at the Hyatt Regency. I got to know Ruth and her husband, Milton, when we were both candidates for the Senate last year. They are two of the best people we met. Milton is the engineer, and Ruth is the politician. She is well on her way to putting him on the Public Utility Commission, where he can do an excellent job for the people of Texas.

We sat at a table with Representative Carolyn Park, who seems to have her head on straight.

This week I served on a jury panel where Judge Jennifer Mattingly brought some unexpected dignity to a Justice of the Peace court.

Women are taking over the government, and I believe it's a good thing. They can't do any worse than the men have done.

April Fool's Prediction: 24% Inflation In 1989

Now that spring has sprung it is time for another prophesy which I expect to dig up and brag about if it turns out right, but only one person is sure to remember if it is wrong.

I bet one of the guys in the office a hundred dollars that inflation in 1989 will be more than twenty per cent. Actually I think it will be closer to twenty four per cent.

Congress is already trying to decide whether the minimum wage will become $4.00 or $4.50. A compromise at $4.25 would be a good guess, more than a twenty five per cent increase.

Those who want to leave it at $3.35 are talking about whether a beginner could be paid the old minimum for a month or six months. In this case the likely compromise is three months, the length of summer vacation.

A foreman supervising ten people will not be satisfied if most of his crew are making more than he is, so it won't take long for the whole increase to filter all the way to the top.

For those of you who don't remember Snead's theorem, it states that more than ninety per cent of anything is labor.

For instance on a road construction job the overall cost is about half labor and half materials. But the sand and gravel used in construction is also about half labor, leaving only about a fourth for materials, such as fuel, explosives, and machinery. But the machinery is also half labor, the other half being steel, which is half labor and half iron ore.

In only five steps labor has accounted for 97 per cent of the cost.

During long periods when the value of money was based on the cost of silver or gold, interest rates on "sure things" were two or three per cent. Our modern high interest rates reflect the money lenders' desire to be repaid in equivalent purchasing power. Fourteen per cent interest actually means twelve per cent for inflation plus two per cent for rent on the money. It will be even more if the lender thinks there is a chance the loan will not be repaid.

Even without taking labor into account, everything necessary to begin a big round of inflation is already under way.

More than a hundred billion dollars has disappeared from American savings banks, and Congress has told the depositors not to worry, "We will see that you get your money somehow."

"Somehow" means either borrowing or printing a hundred billion dollars. You can disregard the part that is supposed to come from the healthy banks. That just makes more money disappear.

If the government has to borrow another hundred billion dollars, the interest rates on government bonds has to increase. It's just a matter of more borrowers courting the same lenders.

The immediate way to put more money in circulation is to lower the Federal Reserve discount rate. This holds interest rates down while allowing inflation to go up, and it is quicker than printing money.

The answer which will irritate voters the least is some borrowing and some new money. Either way there will be much more inflation this year than last year.

So here is Snead's prophesy for April Fool's Day 1989:

The consumer price index will rise between twenty and twenty four per cent in the twelve months ending December 31, 1989.

You can bet on it. I did.

We Can't Afford Religious Fanatics In Government

The recent flap over the Satanic Verses has come at a good time for Americans...that is both North and South Americans.

For more than twelve years we in the north have been enjoying a return to conservative religious values, starting with Jimmy Carter, and continuing with school prayer, the teaching of creation science, and the right to life movement.

Yes, we do need to be reminded that some things are right or wrong regardless of the circumstances, but we also need to be reminded what happens when religious fanatics come into political power.

Five hundred years ago Christians were riding high, and the urgent need to save souls from eternal damnation justified torture to obtain confessions and burning the convicted heretics.

When our Constitution was being written the Inquisition was fairly recent history, and other forms of religious persecution had even more recently driven some of our ancestors to the new world.

Both Thomas Jefferson and Benjamin Franklin were religious, but neither were members of any church. They wanted to assure you and me that any and all churches could flourish in the United States of America, but that none would ever have any political power.

Roughly five hundred years after the founding of the Christian Church, the prophet Mohammed founded Islam. Incidentally, he considered Abraham, Moses and Jesus to be Holy prophets. Now there are probably as many Moslems in the world as there are Christians. The good ones don't drink alcohol, steal or chase women, and they consider the Koran as holy as Christians consider the Bible. They are a good bunch of people.

But the Moslems are giving us a wonderful lesson in what happens when religious leaders come into political power.

This too will pass, but we can't afford to let it happen here.

Keep Plugging Away Doing The Lord's Work

The dozen or so people who read this column regularly will remember that Willie and Joe are spirits who travel all over the universe at the speed of thought, supervising various experiments. There are billions of these guys, but because the distances across the universe are so great, they seldom meet. But they get together occasionally to compare experiences.

Willie and Joe are old hands at this, having been around for thousands of years, but once in a while they have to take time out to indoctrinate a new member like Pete, who has just finished his first tour of duty on one of the inhabitable planets.

Pete is saying, "Hey, Willie, I'm glad to run into you. I'm so frustrated I could almost live again. I've been hanging around that place where I used to live, watching those fools make the same mistakes over and over."

Willie says, "Why are you hanging around there? Don't you know you can go anywhere you like?"

Pete says, "Yeah, God told me that when I first met him. He said I had been doing his work ever since I took my first breath, and now that I've got my honorable discharge I can tackle any project that interests me. I just figured I could do more good back among the people I had lived with, giving them the benefit of my experience."

Willie shrugs and says, "Yeah, that's natural when you don't know anything about the rest of the universe, but it's hard to get them to listen."

Pete says, "You're telling me? I've been watching them try the same dumb things for two hundred years. Every time I try to get a message to one of them, he wants me to pull some hokey miracle to prove I know what I'm talking about."

Willie agrees, "Yeah, I know what you mean. They don't appreciate everyday, useful miracles like healing and photosynthesis. They are only impressed by stunts and entertainment, and when you try to tell them something, they're just not listening."

Pete says, "Yeah, I've noticed that. Even when they are praying, they are likely to be reading from a book. You can't get through until they stop talking and start listening. I've tried to plant some ideas in their dreams, but they don't trust dreams because so many of them are just re-hashes of old fears and bad experiences. They can't tell the good stuff from the bad."

Willie says, "I've planted some pretty good ideas when their minds are blank like right after making love, and I've been able to help sometimes in a crisis. I remember one time when half the people in an airliner were praying for help, and I was able to get the pilot to look at one of the gages that was drifting out of the green. I felt pretty good when the pilot said, "thanks Lord" as he rolled to a stop on the runway. Most of the passengers didn't even know they'd had any help. I had been halfway across the universe when I heard all the commotion and just zipped over to see what I could do."

Pete, remembering a similar experience, suggests, "I'll bet every one of them went right back to making the same dumb mistakes, just like before you saved them."

Willie says, "No, there were one or two including the pilot who were open to some suggestions that made a small difference later on."

But Pete is impatient and cannot understand how Willie can be satisfied with such slow and tedious progress.

But Willie says, "Look, Pete. We've got all the time in the universe. When I first got here the Boss told me that there were no tragic endings for the folks doing his work, and He's not tied to any time table. You're doing a good job, Pete. Just keep plugging away."

A Cynical View Of The U.S. Air Force

I was a second lieutenant in Korea in 1952 and 1953. When I got there I was issued a .45 pistol, a gas mask, and a steel helmet. Every week we had a practice air raid.

The only time I was attacked by an enemy aircraft was one night at an Air Force base near Seoul when "Bed Check Charlie" in an ancient biplane flew over and dropped a couple of hand grenades on us.

When the air raid siren sounded, I hesitated about running outside and crawling into the trench, because I did not have my tin hat with me. After all, I was a visitor on a business trip. Then I noticed that everyone else in the barracks had decided to stay in bed and sleep through the raid.

The next day I learned that if the anti-aircraft guns had started firing on the intruder, the trenches would have been more dangerous than the barracks. Remember, every thing that goes up must come down. (This was before Sputnik.) All the bullets and fragments of shells fired at the enemy aircraft would be stopped or slowed down by the tar paper roof of the barracks.

That night the anti-aircraft gunners also decided to sleep through the raid, so I missed the brilliant display of fireworks that normally greeted the arrival of Bed Check Charlie. Incidentally, our gunners were never able to shoot one down.

I mention all this to give due credit to the F-86 interceptors pilots who made it unprofitable for the North Korean and Chinese Air Forces to attack me and my companions on the ground. The U.S. Air Force did control the sky over Korea, and may have made it possible for me to become a cynical old man rather than a dead, young hero.

The other branch of the Air Force in Korea was not nearly as effective. The F-84 fighter-bombers went out every day loaded to the gills and armed to the teeth, but they were seldom able to find anything to shoot at. I never heard the F-84 pilots brag about hitting any military targets.

The methods they used were not very promising. An infantry officer could not be trusted to direct the work of an Air Force pilot. When a potential target was identified, the

Army had to call for an Air Force officer to drive up in a jeep, look over the situation, and decide if the target was suitable for the Air Force.

If he decided to attack, he would first call in a propeller-driven plane and tell the pilot by radio how to find the target on the ground. The light plane pilot would then shoot a smoke rocket at the target. If all went well, an F-84 would be flying overhead at the right time. The jet pilot would see where the smoke rocket exploded and try to fire the heavy ordinance into the smoke before it drifted away from the target.

After the Korean War the Army pretty much gave up on that kind of help from the Air Force and started arming their helicopters and propeller-driven planes.

Forty years ago airplanes were seldom shot down by ground fire, but the situation has reversed in the last few years. U.S.-made Stinger missiles are given a large part of the credit for driving the Russian helicopters and fighter-bombers out of Afghanistan. Two or three dogfaces with Stinger missiles a mile or two apart have a pretty good chance of shooting down a fifteen million dollar fighter plane which tries to attack any one of them.

Bombing from high altitude is much safer from groundfire, but vulnerable to fighter-interceptors. Furthermore, in combat situations, high altitude bombers have seldom been able to hit anything much smaller than a city.

Of course an Atom Bomb could wipe most of the military targets within an area the size of a small city, but ever since a Russian surface-to-air missile shot down a U-2 spy plane in the late 1950's, high altitude bombing has been something of a suicide mission.

The idea of bombers carrying atom bombs does not fit well with the concept of nuclear war fought with un-manned ballistic and cruise missiles. The war might be over by the time the bombers reach their targets. They might be able to re-arrange the rubble at one end, and not find any place to land when they get home.

Our last, big, successful war was fought without an Air Force. We had an Army Air Corps, and Navy and Marine Air Services. The United States Air Force came into being in

1948 when the U.S. had a monopoly on Atom Bombs, and high altitude bombers were the best way to get them to the targets.

As near as I can tell, the U.S. Air Force is now an organization without a mission. I propose to save a third of our defense budget by holding a huge auction. All of the equipment, personnel, and real estate held by the Air Force would be sold to the highest bidder, with the Army and Navy entitled to the last bid on every item.

Dozens of cities would get new airports, states would get new prisons, and the air lines would get thousands of pilots. Everything left over would be disarmed and recycled into beer cans.

Letter To A Son With A Drug Problem

Dear Son,

Since I didn't get any lessons on "How to be a good Father," I have been just feeling my way along with a little advice from friends now and then.

I wish that I had been smart enough to help you avoid the trap you have fallen into. After the trap was sprung, I have tried to help, but without much success. As you know, my business affairs have been difficult lately, and that has limited the time and money that I have been able to devote to your problem. As it is, the financial cost of your treatments has brought your family to the edge of bankruptcy. Even with the best professional help, your recovery depends mostly on your own strength of character and determination to take charge of your own life.

If your condition continues to get worse, your future is not very bright and is probably short. You could die from an overdose or a silly accident caused by people high on drugs. When we run out of money (and that could be soon) you may have to steal or sell drugs to support your habit. These are dangerous businesses, and lots of the people who practice them are murdered. Those who survive are likely to spend a lot of time in prison. Probably the financial drain on the family will end after the funeral costs or the legal defense fees are paid, but it will not be a happy outcome for any of us.

I would like to offer you an alternative. Since you are old enough to have children of your own, you should learn to be a man.

I am far from perfect, but I have accumulated some experience, both good and bad. I would be pleased to have the opportunity to let you learn from my mistakes and my successes.

You can travel with me for less than the cost of your current treatment. I suggest that we stay together as a working team for as long as it seems to be working. We would eat every meal together, sleep in the same hotel room, exercise together, and make every business contact as a team. After a while you should learn enough to be a real help, and you can probably make some suggestions to improve my effectiveness.

Traveling is lonely work. I would really enjoy having someone I love to keep me company, and it would be a real privilege to be able to pass on what I have learned.

Although you might miss some school, you would be learning how to do what I have done to keep the family eating and living indoors all your life. You may or may not want to follow in my footsteps, but you will be better able to decide after you have walked a few miles in my moccasins.

All in all, my life is a pretty good life. You could make it better for me, and maybe for you too.

A New Welfare System—Three Children Per Family

The other day I read that it may soon be necessary to assign priorities to medical procedures because of the increasing cost of health care and the decreasing amount of money available to pay for it.

This could be a real problem for poor families who are not covered by insurance. The cost of their health care must either be paid by the taxpayers or added to the medical bills of the paying customers.

The author gave an example of the choice between one liver transplant for $150,000 or prenatal and obstetric care for 150 mothers and babies.

Actually, it's not really a difficult choice, but people with the best of intentions would prefer not to have to make the choice, saying, "Surely the leading industrial nation of the world can afford both."

Possibly we could afford the best health care for everyone, regardless of circumstances, if we were not also obligated to be the world's policeman and money lender of last resort, and if there were some reasonable limit on the size of the population entitled to receive the best of everything from cradle to grave.

The engineers of the world have done a pretty nice job of making the world a reasonably good place to live while the rest of the population continues to expand without any apparent limit. We really don't know how many people this planet can support, but we can be sure that there is a limit, and we can reasonably assume that we are approaching the limit pretty fast.

We can also be fairly sure that the earth can support all the people who are living today and all the children they produce if they exercise just a little restraint.

If each woman produced only two children, the population would be stable with a very slight declining trend due to early deaths.

A limit of three children per woman might not be too high, because some women would choose not to raise children at all.

Assuming that a stable population is desirable, our government could do something effective to bring it about within one generation with absolutely no hardship on the citizens who are alive today.

The government could commit itself to unlimited health care and all the other goodies usually associated with U.S. citizenship to all citizens born before January 1st, 1991. This would include all babies conceived before the law went into effect in the Spring of 1990.

After the cut-off date, the standard income tax deduction would be limited to three children per family born after January 1st, 1991.

Similarly, aid to dependent children, which might be called a government subsidy on bastards, would be limited to three per mother born after January 1, 1991.

To help citizens take maximum advantage of the new welfare system, the government could provide sex and birth control education and abortions on demand as part of the unlimited health care available to all citizens living today.

One sticky problem remains. That is what to do about the second class citizens who, through no fault of their own, have three older brothers and sisters. Actually the problem is not as serious as it sounds, because these second class citizens are no worse off than the ordinary citizens of a non-welfare state.

They would know from a very early age that they would have to pay for their own medical care, and might grow into more responsible citizens than their fully-endowed brothers and sisters.

Half of these second class citizens would be women, and they might be much more inclined to limit their own reproduction in order to give their own children a more secure future than they have themselves.

I don't expect this suggestion to be popular. It can only claim to be logical. I could not have even suggested such a thing when I was running for office, but now that I have promised never to do that again, I can run it up the flagpole and see if anybody salutes.

Review Of Freeman Dyson's *Infinite In All Directions*

The most offensive magazine cover I have seen recently was not a picture of hanging hostages or poison gas victims. It was just the words, "TV comes of age. It is the most vital and important cultural force in America. Only snobs, pseudo-intellectuals, and boobs don't recognize the fact."

Since there are many people smarter than me, I am probably not a true intellectual, and since I like to tell people that I don't watch TV, I must be a snob. Boy, the truth hurts!

On the other hand, not watching TV leaves me a lot of time to read books, some just average, but some really good ones. For you true intellectuals who have been too busy watching the boob tube, the best I have read this month is Freeman Dyson's book, *Infinite in All Directions*. Dyson is a professor of physics in the same school as Albert Einstein. He qualifies as a real intellectual.

Dyson writes about relativity, quantum mechanics and astronomy in a way that ordinary snobs can understand. But he also deals with genetic engineering, the origin of life, religion, the Strategic Defense Initiative, nuclear disarmament and space colonies in a way that should not be offensive to any but the most sensitive fanatics.

The surprise is that so many topics seem to fit together in such a satisfying way. A book review is supposed to tell you just enough to make you want to read the book, but maybe it won't be spoiled for you if I quote the last page.

Dyson concludes that in trying to discover the ultimate purpose of the universe, "...the problem is to read God's mind. Previous attempts to read God's mind have not been notably successful. One of the more penetrating of such attempts is recorded in the Book of Job. God's answer to Job out of the whirlwind was not encouraging. Nevertheless I stand in good company when I ask again the questions Job asked. Why do we suffer? Why is the world so unjust? What is the purpose of pain and tragedy? I would like to have answers to these questions, answers which are valid at our childish level of understanding even if they do not penetrate far into the mind of God. My answers are based on a hypothesis which is an extension both of the Anthropic Principle and of the argument from design. The hypothesis is that the universe is constructed according to a principle of maximum diversity. The principle of maximum diversity operates both at the physical and at the mental level. It says that the laws of nature and the initial conditions are such as to make the universe as interesting as possible. As a result, life is possible, but not too easy. Always when things are dull, something new turns up to challenge us and to stop us from settling into a rut. Examples of things which make life difficult are all around us: comet impacts, ice ages, weapons, plagues,nuclear fission, computers, sex, sin and death. Not all challenges can be overcome, and so we have tragedy. Maximum diversity often leads to maximum stress. In the end we survive, but only by the skin of our teeth."

"The expansion of life and of mankind into the universe will lead to a vast diversification of ecologies and of cultures. As in the past, so in the future, the extension of our living space will bring opportunities for tragedy as well as achievement. To this process of growth and diversification I see no end. It is useless for us to try to imagine the varieties of experience, physical and intellectual and religious, to which mankind may attain. To describe the metamorphosis of mankind as we embark on our immense journey into the universe, I return to the humble image of the butterfly. All that can be said was said long ago by Dante in Canto 10 of the Purgatorio:"

> "O you proud Christians, wretched souls and small,
> Who by the dim lights of your twisted minds
> Believe you prosper even as you fall,
> Can you not see that we are worms, each one
> Born to become the angelic butterfly
> That flies defenseless to the Judgment Throne?"

I Don't Watch TV

Jo Anne Ford just acquired a new admirer. When I first met her fifteen years ago she was a counselor at Georgetown High School.

Now she is the principal of the Williams Middle School, and she has just persuaded a third of her students to give up television for almost a week and do a little reading for a change.

This accomplishment is roughly equivalent to getting 170 people to quit smoking for a week. Both smoking and TV are habit-forming. The strain on the kids must have been considerable. But they also must have discovered some nice new things about life, like ex-smokers discover the smell of flowers and the taste of food.

I don't watch TV. When I tell this to my friends, they say, "Yeah, I know what you mean. I only watch the good stuff like PBS and the news and weather."

No, that is not what I mean. I don't watch any of it. Sometimes it leaves me at a serious social disadvantage. I completely miss the point of jokes that are based on the latest TV advertising. I didn't hear the guy sing, "Don't worry...be happy" until it was long past its peak of popularity. I didn't hear about the shooting down of the airliners and the Ayatolla's death sentence until it was too late for me to do anything constructive about them. Incidentally, what did you do?

When somebody at the regular morning coffee klatch asks me what I think about some coach being fired, I have to ask what kind of game he was coaching.

On the other hand, I have my own sins. I read a lot. If I have already read everything else handy, I will sometimes read the phone book...only the yellow pages, of course.

I make a joyful noise on the piano, and I sing in a Barbershop quartet. These things take up a good bit of time, and they keep me out of the pool halls.

I don't listen to the radio either. Sometimes when I am travelling I listen to 'Books on Tape,' and although I know it is hopeless at my age, I have listened to Berlitz tapes on Spanish, French, German, Portuguese and Russian. I know how to ask, "Where is the rest room?" in at least a half dozen languages.

More often I use a tape recorder to dictate these Ex-Candidate's Reports or other ideas that come to me while I am driving. My own voice keeps me awake better than even the most frantic radio announcer.

Getting back to television, we all know the programs and ads are designed for an audience with an 8th grade education, and their main purpose is to get you to want to buy something you didn't even know you needed.

If you want to raise ordinary kids, television probably won't hurt them much. However, if I were still raising kids, I wouldn't have one of the things in my house.

I hope the neighbors would tell me if a tornado was heading my way. The last one missed me anyway.

The Ultimate Cure For Racial Discrimination

I was raised in Austin in the 1930s and 1940s. At that time the only white people who spent much time around colored people were the children. It's not that we were allowed to play with the black kids...most of the white families had colored maids who came to the house almost every day to help with the house work and take care of the children.

Not all of the white folks had cars in those days, and almost none of the blacks had them. I often travelled around Austin with the colored maid, riding in the back of the bus with the rest of the colored folks.

I learned at a tender age that colored people had a distinctive odor, which partially explained to me the rigid segregation which was practiced at that time. Twenty years later I learned that most of the colored people did not have indoor plumbing in their homes, so they seldom took a bath or washed their clothes. I'm sure I smelled much worse when I went three weeks without a bath in Korea. That peculiar, distinctive odor is only a distant memory now.

My father was a building contractor, and by the time I was eight years old he had started teaching me what it means to work. Every summer I worked on one of his construction jobs, and because I had no skills, I worked with the common laborers who were mostly black. There was no minimum wage at that time, but in 1942 I remember the common laborers were paid twenty five cents per hour.

We unloaded bricks from box cars by hand, and mixed mortar for the bricklayers in big wooden tubs that looked like boats. We pulled nails out of used concrete forms, and dug ditches to carefully controlled dimensions to avoid wasting concrete.

One summer I was the smaller half of a two man team with a handsome black man named Pat who taught me to drive a little Caterpillar tractor and to operate a little road grader with big hand wheels which raised and lowered the blade. We took turns operating the road grader and driving the tractor which pulled it.

During the school year I had almost no contact with black people other than our maid and the people on the bus. The black kids went to "separate but equal" schools on the east side of Austin. Actually, we never heard about the "equality" of the schools until the 1950s. We all knew the colored schools were inferior, just like the rest rooms and drinking fountains provided for the colored folks.

Things change slowly. When I first started doing business in Georgetown in 1958 I was surprised to learn that the good people of Georgetown were building another "separate but equal" school several years after the United States Supreme Court had ruled against such schools. Now, of course, Georgetown has one of the most thoroughly integrated school districts in Texas. There is only one school for each age group in town, and bussing is no big deal in a small town.

It is obvious now that our segregated system of the1930s and 40s was wrong. A lot of progress has been made in reducing segregation, but there is still enough discrimination to cause trouble. It is so easy to discriminate. As a matter of fact it is almost impossible not to discriminate. Those black folks just don't look like me and my friends. We just naturally fall into two distinct tribes.

Actually there are more than two tribes in the Austin area which are easily identified by their appearance...the Aztec Indians from Mexico, the blonde and blue-eyed northern Europeans, the light-skinned, dark-haired Mediterraneans, and the almond-eyed Orientals.

All of these tribal characteristics came into existence during long periods of isolation and marriage within the tribes for many generations. Whether we choose to do anything about it or not, the problem will disappear in a few more generations, because the isolation has almost ended.

The TV and motion picture industry will speed up the process by exposing us to more Romeo and Juliet yarns involving people of different races. It could go so far that a scene with two people who look alike in bed together could seem improper and almost incestuous.

I believe like Thomas Jefferson that the government is best which governs least. I would rather see thousands of laws repealed and Congress and the legislatures meet for only a few weeks every two years when it is absolutely necessary, but I seem to be in the minority. Most of the voters seem to believe that anything wrong, anywhere in the world, can and should be cured by government action and taxpayers' money.

If we are going to continue to submit every aspect of our lives to government supervision, then there is an obvious answer to racial discrimination. We can stamp out the differences by selective breeding. Since the government already issues marriage licenses, they could refuse to issue licenses to people whose noses look alike. The justifying theory would be that a thorough mixing of the gene pool would produce superior hybrids. In an few generations we would get used to the idea, and we could take pride in having stamped out skin cancer and sickle cell anemia.

Enthusiasia—The Benevolent World

Willie and Joe, a couple of spirits, are watching a dentist examine a three year old girl, whose baby teeth are almost all rotted away. The dentist is explaining to the child's mother that the decay was caused by the sugar that she put in the baby's bottle over a long period of time.

Joe is saying, "That's the last straw. With all the trouble that can be traced to refined sugar, there ought'a be a law against it."

Willie says, "Yeah, I know how you feel, but over in the Andromeda Galaxy I watched a bunch of people take that kind of thing to its ultimate conclusion."

Joe is indignant. "Hey, you sound like some kind of libertarian freak. People need laws to keep them from making foolish mistakes that can seriously affect their health and welfare."

Willie agrees, "Yeah, they need something to offset their natural foolishness, but I'm not sure that more laws are the answer. Have you ever been over to Enthusiasia in the Andromeda Galaxy?"

There is a flicker of recognition. "No, but I've heard of it. Isn't that the place where they finally got a benevolent world government that was totally dedicated to health and welfare for everybody?"

Willie says, "Yeah, that's the place. I watched them for several hundred years, and it worked like a charm for quite awhile. The vast majority of the people were well disciplined, law abiding, fairly healthy citizens, and a small minority who couldn't or wouldn't shape up went to jail."

Joe nods, "Yeah, I guess there's always going to be a few misfits, even in a perfect system."

Willie held up his hand. "Now wait, I didn't say the system was perfect. There were still lots of people being killed and injured unnecessarily. Victims of their own stupidity, and those that got themselves injured by doing foolish things like jumping out of airplanes and riding motorcycles without a helmet were a burden on the rest of the system, because they sometimes required long term medical care...all at taxpayer expense."

Joe said, "Wait a minute, now that takes a little zing out of life. I've always liked flying myself, that's one of the nicest things about being a spirit. And if a guy wants to knock his brains out riding a motorcycle then that just makes all his other organs available for people that need them."

Willie acknowledges, "What you say is true, but a really benevolent government wants to help people who are too dumb to help themselves. Back in the Milky Way one time I died from lung cancer caused by smoking three packs a day. Maybe if smoking had been illegal or expensive I would have been saved all that agony. They did make it illegal on Enthusiasia, along with everything you could think of that was unhealthy, like refined sugar, saturated fat, alcohol, tranquilizers, driving without seat belts, chain saws, canoes, scuba diving, and swimming without a life jacket."

Joe is impressed, "Wow, I guess everybody must'a lived to be 120 or more, uh?"

"Well," says Willie, "they lived a little longer but it seemed like a lot longer. Especially when it got to where half the people were in jail for things like driving without a seat belt, and taking medicine without a doctor's prescription. The price of all of the prohibited things went out of sight, but you could always get 'em on the black market. Every time they caught a black marketer and put him in jail the prices went up more, making business better for the rest of the black marketers."

Joe said, "Well, I guess a good stiff sentence reformed some of those guys, uh?"

Willie said, "Well, it might have if time in jail was something to be avoided at all costs, but the benevolent government in Enthusiasia figured that anybody in jail was there because of a failure of society, and they could be reeducated and reformed. So, jails got to be more like going back to college but with free room and board, entertainment and exercise."

Joe's amazed, "Gosh, if half of the people were in jail, who paid for the jail and the people to keep them in there?"

"Paid," Willie said, "oh, it didn't cost anything. The government paid for it. They just borrowed money from the rich folks, and when the loans came due they just printed money."

Joe was delighted. "Wow, what a slick system. I can't wait to tell the people back in the Milky Way Galaxy."

Willie shrugs. "Don't bother, they've already heard about it."

High Speed Rail And A High Speed Toll Road
November 3, 1989

Just this last summer, our Texas Legislature passed *The Texas High Speed Rail Act* to enable private businessmen to build a 200 mile per hour passenger train system between Fort Worth, Dallas, Houston, San Antonio and Austin.

A board of nine people familiar with transportation will review the proposals received and decide which group should receive the franchise that would give them the right to buy the needed land for right–of–way.

Robert C. Lanier, retired chairman of the State Highway and Public Transportation Commission and Robert H. Dedman, its present chairman, along with Clive Runnels, head of the Texas Turnpike Authority, Kent Hance, chairman of the Texas Railroad Commission, and David McCall, with Dallas Area Rapid Transit will be on the board.

Just recently Governor Clements added D. Kent Anderson, a Houston banker, and sometime soon he will appoint three others before the board becomes effective.

The idea is to provide Texans with trains similar to but faster than those in Germany, France and Japan, provided they can be built and operated on the money collected from ticket sales.

I have been in the railroad business for 31 years, and am fascinated by the project. The proposed trains could get us from Austin to Dallas almost as quickly as existing air lines and would burn only one fifth as much petroleum. They could also run on electricity produced by clean burning Texas natural gas.

All of the trains being proposed, the German Inter City Express, which they like to call the ICE of Texas (get it?), the Shin Kan Sen, meaning New Trunk Line, are state of the art equipment with steel wheels running on standard gauge rails, generally compatible with our existing railway system.

In July I rode the German Inter City Express at 175 miles per hour, and got a close look at their new Magnetic Levitation train. I had been skeptical about magnetic levitation until I toured the research center and saw the train in operation. I came away converted...a new believer in the train of the future. It has already demonstrated a top speed of 257 miles per hour, and it is designed for 310 mph. It can start and stop quicker than ordinary trains and climb a ten percent grade, compared to two percent for trains with wheels. There is none of the usual train noise as it goes by, just a variable pitch song or whistle like you would expect from a flying saucer from outer space.

One of the largest contractors in the United States is ready to build a Mag–Lev track from Los Angeles to Las Vegas and have it in operation in five years. I would dearly love to have one running in Texas before California gets one.

My only reservation is whether these trains can be a good deal for a businessman to build and operate. The 200 mph wheel–on–rail system from Dallas to Houston is expected to cost about 2.5 billion dollars, and the Mag–Lev version might cost twice as much.

The tickets would probably have to be priced a little below the airline fares, but I have some doubt whether enough tickets can be sold at this price to pay off the construction bonds plus operation costs, with enough left over to make it interesting to a businessman.

On the other hand, I believe the project should be started immediately if is at all possible. Existing railroads and interstate highways have many curves that are too tight for 200 and 300 mph vehicles, so new right-of-way must be acquired away from built up areas. And it should be bought NOW while Texas land is the cheapest it has been in the last ten years.

Since I also believe we are in for another big round of inflation, this land should double in value in the next five years. A person with money to invest could put it in land reserved for Texas High Speed Rail System now with reasonable confidence that it would be worth more five years from now than money put in government bonds, even if the high speed railways are not built until much later.

I am afraid it will take a long time to change the driving habits of Texans, especially if gasoline prices stay low. The majority will continue driving between Ft. Worth, Dallas, Houston, San Antonio and Austin, knowing that their driving cost is a little more than airline and train tickets.

The people pushing the high speed trains make a big thing about going from downtown Austin to downtown Dallas, but they overlook the fact that most Austin people don't live downtown, and for most trips the destination is not downtown either, so there is likely to be need for driving a car at both ends. So as long as gasoline is cheap and Texans are prosperous, I believe they are going to continue to drive their cars.

That brings us to an interim, money making idea for the high speed right–of–way that's to be acquired now for trains to use ten to fifteen years in the future. Why not build toll roads on which it would safe (and legal) to drive 100 mph or more? The availability of high speed roads would create a new market for expensive cars that can be driven safely at high speeds.

Later, each high speed automobile could be equipped with a transponder to identify itself and authorized drivers, and fiber optic cables could be run all along the route to facilitate collecting toll charges by mail, enforce speed limits, and periodically check drivers for alertness and sobriety. The same fiber optic system could later be used for centralized train control.

When the price of gasoline finally gets high enough, and Texas' population demands it, the German Mag–Lev train will be ready to boost our travel speed safely to 300 mph on the same roadways we had the foresight to buy when land was cheap back in 1989.

Now I Need Your Help

I am about to take an active part in this project which will cost me enough to hurt if I have guessed wrong about the attitude of Texans toward automobiles, roads, trains and airplanes. There are 60,000 people who might read this article. If you have read this far and have an opinion on the subject, I would really like to hear from you. Please call my office in Georgetown, at 1–512–863–5881 and tell what you think about it. Your opinion could have a real bearing on when and if this project gets underway. I look forward to hearing from you.

Ned Snead

Legalization is the Best War Against Drugs

Some of my best friends are unusual people like Marion Griffith, Mike Zuteck, and Homer Phillips. They are likely to send me an envelope full of newspaper clippings without any comments or anything to indicate where they came from or who sent them.

This one must have come from Homer Phillips, because it was apparently printed in the *San Antonio Light*, but it was written by Mike Royko, who is a columnist with the *Chicago Tribune*. I believe it is timely, because it deals with one of the problems covered in a recent *Austin Weekly* cover story about violence on East Sixth Street.

Mike says, "John is a white Chicago cop. He doesn't want his full name used because what he has to say might not please his superiors, although many probably agree with him.

> I'm a sergeant, and I've worked on the West Side by choice most of my career. So I know something about the problem of drugs. I think I know more about it than some of the people who do a lot of talking about winning the drug war and make the laws and set our national policies, but have never been on the street where everything is happening.
>
> For years I've been advocating, mostly to my friends, the legalization of drugs and using the billions we'd save from trying to fight the import and sales to cure those who want to be cured.
>
> The way things go now, the courts will sentence drug offenders and people who steal to get drug money to rehabilitation as a condition of probation.
>
> But what happens when they want to go straight and can't get into a program for six months, which is very common? I'll tell you what. They go right back to their friends and habits.
>
> On the West Side, kids complain that we stopped them because they were Black and driving a Cadillac. That was true. Most often the car was stolen and we had to chase them.
>
> But now that's changed. Now the cars belong to them, and they've paid cash. And some of them aren't even old enough to drive.

> Those of us in law enforcement look like fools trying to fight a battle we can't win. And that just breeds contempt for law and order. Even if we were able to stop the coke from Colombia and Peru, it wouldn't change things. It would come in from somewhere else. And if we stopped that, it still wouldn't change because they can make this synthetic stuff right here. They're doing it already.
>
> The problem is the demand. And the only thing for sure is that where there is a demand, it will be satisfied. That's a basic market principle, and that's why all the arguments against legalizing and controlling drugs are nonsense.
>
> We have 13-year-old dealers who make more than me. They go out and sell, then it will likely have a familiar result: failure. They give some of the money to Mom, who maybe lives in the Chicago Housing Authority or some dump. She needs it to make ends meet. How can President Bush fault someone who lives in a drafty apartment and is wanting for food and has no chance for a decent education or a job for selling drugs? How are you going to convince the kids to get back to school so they can be a factory worker, or get a low-paying job in a fast food place, or be unemployed, when they can sell drugs for big money?
>
> The way we're going at this thing reminds me of Vietnam. A quagmire. Lives lost, then we pack up and leave.
>
> One of the reasons we study history is to learn from our own mistakes. Well, it looks like we didn't learn anything from Prohibition.
>
> I keep reading that every poll shows that most people who get polled are against any kind of legalizing of drugs.
>
> You know what that tells me? It tells me that most people who get polled don't know what the hell is going on out here."

Mike Royko continues, "That's one cop's opinion. But I suspect it is also the opinion of thousands of other cops in Chicago, New York, Los Angeles and in most cities where the problems are the same.

"Since they're the ones who are actually fighting this no-win war, I respect their opinions more than the word warriors in Washington who have never been any closer to Chicago's

West Side, or New York's Bronx or Los Angeles' Watts than their TV sets can get them."

That says it better than anything I could say. The headline in the *San Antonio Light* said, "DRUG FIGHTER ON THE FRONT LINES BELIEVES LEGALIZATION IS OUR BEST HOPE."

Voters Need To Come Up With Answers
December 8 , 1989

To the Editor of the *Austin Weekly*

Kirk Becker and John H. Gellasch have done more for me than they might know. First, it is nice to know that somebody is reading my column, and second, they have called attention to the fact that my article on population "...raised more questions than it answers."

I would never suggest a federally enforced limit on the number of children a woman could bear, although this is mentioned almost exactly in both letters. I will always believe that the government is best which governs least.

I believe our government is the source of most of our problems, even while our lawmakers are trying with the best of intentions to solve problems.

The children of large families are the innocent victims of careless parents, particularly in cases where the parents are in poor financial condition. A forty-acre farm and a ten thousand dollar insurance policy don't amount to much when they are divided among ten kids.

In their efforts to help the innocent victims of excessive breeding, our government ends up by subsidizing large families. If you can deliver that baby before December 31st, it's worth an extra income tax deduction. If you're an unwed teen-age mother, and you have another baby, you can get a bigger monthly check for aid to dependent children.

Who is it that wants to insist that an unwed teen-age girl deliver and care for a baby for twenty years? Certainly not her mother. Maybe it's someone who has long-term plans to build up a bigger voting bloc. Maybe it's someone who wants her to suffer for her sins. Certainly it is not someone who is trying to figure out how to pay for all the government services we have already voted for.

You and I are not obligated to provide homes for all the kittens and puppies that might appear. Years ago in Houston I knew a lady who thought she could and tried. She was a little crazy, but at least she worked on the problem with her own money.

Kirk and John are both right. I don't have it all figured out, but I am not alone in that. Our lawmakers are really not to blame either. They must do what the voters tell them if they want to keep on being lawmakers. This is our country. Those guys work for us. We can't just keep on finding problems for our leaders to throw money at. Let's try to give them some answers.

Answer To An Unsigned Letter

A few days ago I received an unsigned letter from a lady, judging from the neat handwriting. She was assured of a place in Heaven herself, but she was concerned about my soul because I obviously, "think I am smarter than God."

Since there was no return address, I will have to use this column to assure her that I only think I am smarter than some of the priests who claim to speak for God.

About ten years ago I was ordained as a priest myself in one of the less well known denominations. Since I have not received anything to indicate that I have been excommunicated, I assume that I still have some limited access to revelations.

Of course, I can't prove that my revelations come direct from God, because He doesn't make a big fuss over them like burning up a roadside bush. They just leave me with an unshakable faith that requires no further proof. A couple of examples might be helpful:

On Christmas day about twenty years ago, while watching television pictures of the Moon taken from lunar orbit, I became convinced that we are totally alone in the universe. I was not at all surprised when a later spacecraft was not able to find any evidence of life on Mars. I also have absolutely no interest in the Search for Extra Terrestrial Intelligence (SETI). I recently learned from a mutual friend that Carl Sagan didn't either until he learned from public opinion polls that the majority of the public supports the effort. That's the mark of a real politician.

Another revelation came quietly while reading about Hinduism and Mahatma Gandhi. The most thoughtful Hindus will not belittle any man's religion if it seems to be doing him any good. They say that there are many roads starting at the bottom of the mountain, but they all lead to the same point at the top.

Any knowledge we have, particularly that which comes directly from God, must result in action if it is to be more than just interesting conversation. If we really are alone in the universe, then life here is far more precious than it would be if this were only one of many of God's experiments.

However, since every plant and animal will be dead in a few years anyway, our duty is not to preserve individuals, but to preserve life on Earth, and particularly human life, since it appears to us to be God's most successful experiment to date.

The revelation about religion tells me that regardless of how sure I am about my own faith, I should not push it on others. If anyone should notice my halo and ask me what it is that makes me such a wonderful guy, then I can tell them about my religion. So far it hasn't happened.

Buy American—North And South
December 19, 1989

American oil companies are buying crude petroleum from the Persian Gulf because that is the cheapest source.

At one time Persian Gulf oil was REALLY CHEAP because it reflected the cost of production. Since the Arab nations have taken over the ownership of the oil wells, they have apparently tried to set prices to yield the maximum number of dollars per year, or possibly per barrel of reserves.

We should be familiar with the pricing method from our experience with AMTRAK, whose president has told reporters that ticket prices are not related to cost of service. He believes that if prices were lowered he would sell more tickets but receive less total revenue. On the other hand, if he raised prices he would sell fewer tickets and again receive less total revenue.

In the case of AMTRAK, neither tactic would cover the cost of operation, but if he finds the optimum price, he will be able to minimize the losses to be covered by the taxpayers.

The Persian Gulf situation is similar, but opposite. The cost of production is covered many times over, but with optimum pricing the dollar yield is maximized.

Under current prices I believe the price of Arab oil is just enough lower than Texas, Mexico and Venezuela prices to offset the cost of production and transportation and possibly the differential yield of marketable products.

Ten or fifteen years ago, with oil prices high and rising, there was apparent prosperity in Latin America, which led to investments and loans to be repaid out of oil profits.

Now with oil prices too low for Texas, Mexico and Venezuela to compete in the market, the expected oil profits have turned to losses, and the loans made by North American banks have gone sour, contributing to bank failures. Mexico and Venezuela are two of the prominent Latin American nations which are far behind on the payments to North American banks.

There is a real possibility that many Latin American nations, under pressure from their citizens and voters, will stop all payments on these loans. To counter this possibility, there is a growing consensus here that some portion, possibly a third, of these loans should be forgiven.

At first glance it is no big deal to forgive a loan that you will never be able to collect anyway. However, with a bank writes off a bad loan it also reduces its taxable income. So even if the bank survives, at least a third of the amount forgiven is paid by the taxpayers. That's the good news.

If the bank fails as a result of writing off too many bad loans, then the entire loss falls on the taxpayers, because most deposits are insured by the taxpayers.

So now we have a fairly complete picture of another example of the government's right hand not knowing what the left hand is doing. By refusing to restrict oil imports from the Persian Gulf we impoverish two potentially prosperous Latin American neighbors and let the taxpayers pick up the tab for the government's bad judgement.

We are sending unbelievable amounts of money to the Persian Gulf, far more than they can spend locally. To prove to the Arabs that the dollars we send them have real value, we must sell them things of real value like North American hotels, factories and land...that is when they get tired of kingly toys like jet fighters and stinger missiles.

If I were a devout Muslim chief of state, I could not in my wildest dreams have imagined a more satisfactory way to bring "the Great Satan" to its knees.

I don't like to point out problems without offering solutions, so here is at least a start.

A federal tax (or if you are a lip reader,* an import fee) on oil imported from anywhere other than North and South America. The money raised could be used to reduce the federal deficit or to subsidize imports from the Americas.

Oil-producing Latin American countries could pay their debts to North American bankers in shiploads or trainloads of oil, which would be sold to North American refineries for cash.

When Kent Hance crashed a meeting of O.P.E.C. (the Organization of Petroleum Exporting Countries), he claimed to represent Texas as the fourth largest oil-producing 'nation' in the world. Anything along this line we can do for Mexico and Venezuela will also be good for Texas.

*A reference to George Bush's campaign promise, "Read my lips, no new taxes."

Noriega And The Evil Empire

A guy who doesn't watch TV and only reads weekly newspapers and magazines leaves himself open for a surprise once in a while.

The other day I learned at the Georgetown Rock Crushers' Dawn Coffee Klatch that the good old U.S. of A. is at war again. What a relief! I had been worrying about what I was going to do about the hundreds of thousands of Texans who have been building jet fighters and stinger missiles who would be out of work because of peace breaking out in Europe.

Every modern government for the last 2,000 years has needed a thoroughly evil enemy to justify high taxes and Big Brother type control over citizens' affairs. How lucky we are to have one right under our noses that we can probably whip without too much loss of life and treasure!

The new enemy leader is the perfect example of evil incarnate. He has gotten filthy rich selling drugs to North American teen-age children. In his photographs he looks evil, because his face was scarred by a childhood disease. He also refuses to salute high North American officers and to pledge allegiance to The Flag.

We are fortunate to have 20,000 or more troops already stationed in Panama, although that will probably not be enough in the long run to defeat a private army financed by North American drug addicts. We may also have some trouble reminding the natives that we are the good guys after three years of economic sanctions which had no effect on the evil empire while it wrecked the civilian economy.

No doubt justice will triumph in the end like it did in the Falkland Islands and Grenada.

It's a shame we have had to put a million-dollar bounty on the leader's head. It's necessary, of course, if it saves even a few of our soldiers from unnecessary death or injury. After all, the rules are different in war. Even so, the spirit of Ayatollah Khomeini must be getting a chuckle.

It's really going to be embarrassing if more than one bounty hunter shows up with a bloody, pock-marked head.

Financing The High Speed Railroad

A couple of months ago I wrote an article about a high speed passenger train system to connect Fort Worth, Dallas, Houston, Austin and San Antonio. At that time I said that if the system were in service now, it would not bring in enough money from ticket sales to pay for both the operating and construction costs.

However, I also said that the land for the right-of-way, with the long, smooth curves necessary for 200 mph trains should be purchased now, while Texas land is cheaper than it has been for the last ten years. The key question is how to pay for the land while we wait for the price of gasoline to rise and for passenger trains to become an economic necessity.

Some have suggested that we "let the government help" with the cost. In my experience government help comes with so many strings attached that the extra cost more than eats up the money provided by the government. Our government seems to be able to foul up a two-car funeral.

My solution is to acquire a wider right-of-way than the minimum needed for trains, for instance 400 feet, and immediately build a toll road where high-performance automobiles can be driven legally and safely at 100 miles per hour or more. I firmly believe that such a highway could pay for itself out of tolls collected in just a few years. Later, when passenger trains become a necessity, the tracks could be built on one or two lanes of the existing toll road, taking advantage of all the bridges and other expensive features which would be already in place.

Lots of people have told me that it sounds like a good idea, but Chris Putsche, one of my low-brow friends, told me that "Ideas are like hemorrhoids. Sooner or later everybody gets one." The question is, "How can we turn a good idea into a worthwhile, money-making project without it being a burden on the taxpayers?"

How about this? All through this century Texas land has been increasing in market value on a long-term trend of about 13 per cent per year. However, the current prices of Texas land, when it actually sells, is less than it was five years ago. With an increase in the federal minimum wage scheduled for 1990, inflation could be just around the corner. Folk wisdom has always said that land is the best possible long-term investment and hedge against inflation.

I suggest raising about sixty million dollars immediately for the purchase of right-of-way between Houston and Dallas, financed by bonds secured by a first mortgage on a long, narrow strip of Texas land.

The bonds would earn interest at a higher rate than certificates of deposit, but instead of being paid in cash, the interest would be added to the principal. No payments would be made on the principal until construction starts, at which time the whole amount including accrued interest would be paid.

In order to ease the financing of construction, the right-of-way bonds could be issued to individually cover only certain sections of the roadway, for instance from one small town to another, where entrances, exits, and toll plazas might be located.

The right-of-way bonds might also carry the privilege of conversion to stock in the toll road corporation at a favorable price.

Another possibility is the conversion of the right-of-way bonds into revenue bonds which could earn a share of the revenue collected on only certain sections of the road. In this computer age it would be fairly easy to determine how much money was collected on each section of the road in order to pay the bond holder his share.

Any type of public transportation system will always have more activity on some sections of the network, and these sections will be the easiest to finance. But there will always be pressure from certain cities and towns to be included in the system before they are economically feasible. The availability of bonds covering only certain sections of the road would make it easy for local businessmen and politicians to "put their money where their mouth is" and bring the toll road or the high speed trains into their favorite area, even if it takes a little longer to pay off the bonds.

The last time I wrote an article on this subject I asked for comments from the readers, and received several dozen letters, all of them favorable, with only a few expressing concern about the safety of driving 150 mph. I would like to hear from the readers again, especially those who know more about money and finance than I do.

Downtown Airports Are Priceless

I learned to fly in Dallas in 1944. My dad had done a paving job for Lou Foote who was training civilian pilots while they waited for a class in the Army flight training program. When the U.S.A. started winning the war the Army quit paying Lou for training pilots, which made it hard for Lou to pay my dad for the paving, so both Pop and I learned to fly at Lou Foote's expense.

Pop bought and sold (or crashed) several airplanes in the next few years, and by the time I got back from the Korean war he was keeping his plane in Bobby Ragsdale's hangar number one at Robert Mueller Airport.

Radios were lousy in those days, and the tower was still using red and green light guns to control traffic. In the late 1960s my brother Bill and I flew our Schweizer TG-2 glider out of there and Bergstrom.

At that time a Cessna 180 could almost keep up with a DC-3 and could frequently beat the airlines to Chicago or Washington, D.C., and always to Pana, Illinois or Hinesville, Georgia.

With the airlines doing 500 mph now it is more difficult for a businessman to justify flying his own airplane, particularly if he has to fly into mad houses like Houston Intercontinental or DFW. When I fly to Houston, I land at Lakeside or Hobby, and in Dallas I land at Redbird or Love.

These downtown airports are priceless to general aviation, and general aviation will be bringing in money to Austin long after the Air Force has quit being a big local employer.

You can land big airplanes on small airports, because they are light when they have burned most of their fuel. The problem is taking off when they are loaded with passengers and fuel for a flight to Europe. Bergstrom is a perfect place for trans-continental flights. Even if the Air Force stays, they don't fly much. If a big war breaks out, all the civilian flights will be controlled by the Air Force anyway.

The idea of conflicts between the traffic at Mueller and Bergstrom is mostly hogwash. All air traffic into the Austin area is controlled by Austin Approach Radar.

A Common Sense Approach To Outer Space

Hubert (Grade-Point) Davis was the smartest kid in my class of Mechanical Engineering students at Texas A & M. After our service in the Korean war Hubert became one of the first engineers at NASA's Manned Spaceflight Center in Houston. He was project manager on the Lunar Excursion Module which landed Neil Armstrong and Buzz Aldrin on the moon ahead of schedule.

Nearly everybody involved in the space program is smart, but Davis is like a breath of fresh air among some of the "far-out" science fiction types. He likes the term, "hillbilly engineering" and can often suggest a mass-produced auto part or hardware store item in place of the exotic and fantastically expensive gadgets that rocket scientists love to design.

A few years ago the wreck of the Space Shuttle, Challenger, brought him out of early retirement mad as a wet hen, remembering arguments he had lost when the Shuttle was first being designed.

The Shuttle is a magnificent flying machine for getting men with their tools and spare parts to and from their work in low earth orbit. But the idea of the Shuttle being a "truck" which could haul anything and everything is ridiculous. It is like using a Winnebago to haul bricks and mortar to a construction site.

The heavy hauling needs to be done by a specialized piece of equipment analogous to a truck or freight car, with a minimum crew. If possible, it should be unmanned.

The Space Shuttle's main engines are one of NASA's masterpieces. They are the most efficient rocket engines in service, and they burn only hydrogen and oxygen, producing only water vapor in the exhaust jet. They are also extremely expensive, costing many millions of dollars each.

By contrast, the solid rocket boosters, also used on the Shuttle, are crude, inefficient and dangerous. One of them was the direct cause of the Challenger explosion. They produce tons of noxious gasses including hydrochloric acid.

Davis has designed a family of unmanned, heavy lift freight rockets using only the well proven Space Shuttle Main

Engines and a unique system for bringing home these expensive jewels by ram air inflated parachutes like those now used by sport jumpers. The engines would be caught by arresting gear on ships at sea or snatched from the air by helicopters and returned to the launching site for reuse without ever being bumped on the ground or dipped in sea water. Cheaper elements like fuel tanks could be discarded and still let the system put its payload in orbit at much lower cost than anything existing or proposed in the U.S. Space Program.

Davis calls his system the "CONSORT," because it is an unmanned companion vehicle to the Shuttle, using the same major components and launch facilities. The higher utilization would result in lower cost for both systems.

Much of the public debate recently has revolved around whether the U.S. Space Program should provide for our Strategic Defense, electric power from sunlight, a trip to Mars, an outpost on the moon, or a permanent manned space station. Regardless of which you prefer, the immediate need is for a cheaper way to get materials into low earth orbit. This is essential to "all of the above."

Twenty years ago the U.S.A. was the undisputed leader in space. In the last few years the Soviets have launched ten times as many space flights as the U.S.A., the French have taken over the commercial satellite business, and the Japanese are launching sophisticated space research vehicles.

I have had dozens of conversations with space professionals without hearing of anything more practical than Davis' CONSORT proposal. It is time for the U.S. Space Program to get back in high gear, and if they can't beat the CONSORT, they should build it.

The Sign Dictionary

As long as I can remember I have been fascinated, but frustrated, by foreign languages. I am one of the people who learn primarily by what I see. What I hear is frequently forgotten before the echo dies.

By working hard I have learned a few key phrases like, "Do you speak English?" in Spanish, French, German, Chinese and Japanese, but only in Spanish can I even begin to carry on a simple conversation.

I have long believed that free trade is the surest way to world peace, and that languages are the greatest obstacles to world trade. I also believe that all languages are unnecessarily complex.

Back in the early 1970s someone told me that a thousand–word vocabulary was enough for any language. Then Wallace Giddings, a Georgetown friend, told me that during World War II he had worked on a project to translate some Army radar manuals into a Basic English vocabulary of less than a thousand words for the benefit of some Chinese technicians.

Bill Jones, a professor at Southwestern University, helped me to track down Charles Kay Ogden, the Cambridge professor who originated the idea of Basic English in the 1930's. He selected a list of 850 English words and demonstrated their power by translating parts of the Bible and several classics of English literature into Basic English. For technical use, he allowed 150 additional words in each specialty, bringing the total back up to the magic one thousand.

The Caterpillar Tractor Company and Bell Helicopter have made effective use of Ogden's idea recently by translating some of their equipment maintenance manuals into "Caterpillar Fundamental English" using a slightly different word list.

I learned that Japanese newspapers and magazines had standardized on 1,850 of the old Chinese characters to be used in all Japanese typesetting machines, in addition to the 40 phonetic characters called Kata Kana and Hira Gana. The 1,850 Toyo Kanji are divided into seven groups to be taught to Japanese students their first six years in school, and a final set to be learned in junior high school.

I spent more time than I like to admit digging through a Chinese/Japanese dictionary trying to match up the Toyo Kanji with Ogden's and Caterpillar's lists. Only about half of the words matched.

Later while travelling through California with my daughter, Dr. Bonnie Stump, and her husband, Bill, I was killing time in a University library, and I found a book by Mario Pei entitled, *One Language for the World.* Pei was not pushing any particular language. He simply proposed that all the nations of the world call a convention for the purpose of selecting an auxiliary language, natural or artificial, to be taught to all children in addition to their native language, beginning with their first school year. In only one generation the language problems of the world would disappear.

When I got home I tried to locate Mario Pei, and found that he had died at almost the same time I discovered his book. It was almost as if he was waiting to move on to his next assignment until someone picked up the torch he had been carrying.

My idea was to carry Mario Pei's idea to Rotary International, an organization of a million men and women all over the world dedicated to peace through the productive work of business and professional people.

Mario Pei's book was out of print, and I bought all of the few dozen remaining copies and sent one to each of the officers and directors of Rotary International. Then I went to the Rotary meeting in Chicago and Sao Paulo, Brazil trying to persuade the top brass to promote the international language convention. I got a few polite hearings, but no action.

To demonstrate how it could be done, the Georgetown Rotary Club held a mock convention at Southwestern University. About fifty people attended, representing more than a dozen candidate languages, and in two days of debate, narrowed the choices down to Swahili and Esperanto. We learned that our voting system was flawed, and the flaw was quickly discovered by the group supporting Esperanto, and they used it to their advantage. We'll do better if we have another convention.

The leader of the Russian delegation was Claude Proctor, who had been a language expert in the U.S. Air Force. When it became obvious that Rotary International was not going to support the language convention idea, Claude and I decided to tackle a more modest project.

My daughter, Jeannie Sutton, is a registered interpreter for the deaf, and competent in American Sign Language (Ameslan). Her books made it obvious that the basic Ameslan vocabulary is about two thousand words, in general agreement with Ogden's Basic English and the Japanese Toyo Kanji. Claude and I concluded that Sign Language might be acceptable as an international auxiliary language. It avoids most of the imperial overtones and can be useful in some situations which are not served by normal written and spoken languages. For example, underwater divers, around noisy construction sites and around airplanes and helicopters, for conversations across crowded rooms, or even behind the teacher's back.

Claude set to work making his own "core vocabulary" list of the most essential words in any language, mostly disregarding previous work. He located Tony L. McGregor, who was hearing impaired from birth, to do the art work to illustrate the 2,400 words that he had selected.

Proctor also spent a couple of years looking up words in dozens of dictionaries to be sure that the essential meaning of each word could be found in each of the fourteen languages he considered most important in the modern world. His list included American Sign Language, Arabic, Chinese, Dutch, English, French, German, Italian, Japanese, Korean, Portuguese, Russian, Spanish and Swedish. I regret that we were not able to include Hindi, Urdu, and Farsi, but of course, wherever you draw the line, someone will be disappointed.

For a time we had the enthusiastic support of Gallaudet University, the only four–year college for the deaf in the world. These people made some valuable suggestions and contributed about ten thousand dollars to the cost of the typesetting, but an internal fight between the library and the public relations department ended their participation.

However, the Georgetown Rotary Club had gone too far to turn back. The individual members of the club have volunteered to underwrite all the remaining costs to get the *Illustrated Dictionary* printed and into the hands of the public.

The final preparation of the camera ready copy and the printing are being done by Hart Graphics in Austin. The first run will be 3,500 copies. The books are about the size of a Texas Almanac, and will sell for $19.95. There are about 600 pages of sign language illustrations with each sign translated into the thirteen languages. There are thirteen separate alphabetized indexes.

The book should be helpful for those wanting to learn sign language, and for travellers or business people who need to send or receive simple messages. Of course, no one will be able to master a language just reading a dictionary. But, the Georgetown Rotary Club's *Illustrated International Dictionary* is unique in all the world and will serve as a symbol of both the necessity and the possibility of learning to work together in peace with people all over the world.

A Story Of How Underdogs Live And Die

A few weeks ago my son–in–law gave me a copy of Salman Rushdie's book, *Satanic Verses.* I had been curious about it ever since the big flap over the price on the author's head, but not enough to go out and buy a copy.

Parts of the book were interesting to me, because much of the action takes place in Bombay and London, both cities I have visited. The author also introduces a much wider variety of characters than a tourist or businessman is likely to meet, all probably true to life.

The many characters display a wide variety of attitudes, from pious to contemptuous, toward the major religions encountered by Indians at home and aborad. In principle a Hindu should be tolerant of all varieties of religious faith. "Many roads start at the foot of the mountain, all leading to the same place at the top." Their leaders tell them not to make fun of anyone's religion, if it seems to be doing him any good.

Rushdie spares no one, but in the process of poking fun at Hindus, Moslems, Christians and Jews he tells many stories that would be unfamiliar to people whose experience is confined to only one of these powerful faiths. If religion were not such a sensitive subject, his work would illustrate how alike we all are, both in our noble ideals and in our foolish actions. Apparently some people just can't take a joke.

The whole book concerns the adventures of two men who are miraculously saved after their airliner explodes at 30,000 feet over the English Channel. One turns into an archangel and the other into a devil. Most of the action takes place within the dreams of these two men, but it is difficult for the reader to know which are the dreams of the characters and which are the dreams of the author. Outrageous things happen in both cases.

Satanic Verses is not an easy book to read. Places and things are mentioned casually with English spelling of Indian names, and the dialog is peppered with inside jokes, jargon and verbatim stuttering. Many lines have to be read two or three times, and sometimes skipped over as hopeless.

Much of the story is colored by the difficulties tolerated by dark skinned people living in a world dominated by the light skinned. There are no heros. Every major character is repeatedly frustrated and dies tragically without meaning.

There is plenty of sex, not particularly descriptive, but meaningless and frustrating. The book could be a pretty good description of the way underdogs live and die when they are not supported by any effective religious faith.

I kept reading to the end, because I wanted to know what was so offensive to the late Ayatollah Khomeni. There are two characters set in dreams where a thinly disguised Prophet leading a small band of worshipers of the one and only God seeks advice from an archangel and sometimes comes back with revelations which are more distinguished for their political expediency than for their religious piety.

Similar stories could be and have been written around the sacred scriptures of the Jews, Christians, Mormons, and Hindus. To me the *Satanic Verses* seemed no worse than *Jesus Christ, Superstar.*

I really can't recommend the book. There are plenty of other books in English which would help us to learn enough about Islam to deal effectively and peacefully with those who "submit to the Will of God." An example would be the autobiography, *Daughter of Destiny* by Benzir Bhutto, prime minister of Pakistan.

Only The Dead Have Seen The Last Of War

The last couple of years have been an exciting and amazing time for a peace lover. When I was campaigning for the Senate in 1988 I frequently met with people eager to support the war in Nicaragua, build radar proof bombers, and deploy lethal weapons in space. The Soviet threat which was the original reason for these things seems to be dissolving like a bad dream.

Peace does seem to be breaking out all over, but at times like these we need to be reminded of what Plato said more than 2,000 years ago, "Only the dead have seen the last of war."

Lately I have been reading William Manchester's book, *The Last Lion: Winston Spencer Churchill: 1932-1940.* He reminds us that in the 1920s and 1930s the English and French were really sick of war, much more than we are today after Vietnam. They had lost millions of young men in mindless, stagnant trench warfare, and they had imposed severe restrictions on Germany's armaments in the Treaty of Versailles. Their mood was, "Never again.... Universal disarmament.... Beat swords into plowshares and study war no more."

Only the Germans, a proud race of 'supermen' who believed they had been treated unfairly at Versailles, still retained the spirit and the will to fight. Hitler appealed to the pride and the frustration of these technically skilled and well disciplined people and led them, slowly at first, to disregard the Treaty and build the largest war machine the world had ever seen.

Probably the French or the English could have stopped the German build-up before it was too late by a show of force and determination, but the people and their leaders were so repelled by the thought of war that they lacked the guts even to bluff effectively. They hoped they could negotiate with Hitler.

Their excessive craving for peace led directly to the greatest war of all time.

But before we blame the people of England or France, or even Germany for World War II, we should take a closer look at Adolph Hitler's early followers.

Remember, not only the German army and navy, but the German people were disarmed after World War I. In that environment a young thug armed only with a club or a bicycle chain is a real threat to a middle-aged man or woman. A dozen thugs organized into an effective team are more than a match for a hundred unarmed and disorganized civilians. Two or three policemen armed with pistols could control such a gang, but to be ready 24 hours per day, they must be backed up by four or five times the number patrolling at any one time.

Back in the late 1930s there was a fight in the Brykerwood Elementary School yard almost every day. Fighting seems to come naturally to boys. When they get just a little older they become fascinated by guns, even before they start taking an interest in girls. That is the time for their fathers to teach them how to shoot at targets and to handle guns safely.

A teen-age boy is the ideal soldier. He is used to fighting, he loves guns, and he still believes that bad things only happen to other boys. He knows he can drive a car at any speed because of his superior skill. This is the time when he can easily be recruited into a man's world, be given a rifle and a little infantry training and hustled into battle. He is told that it is mostly the clumsy and cowardly who are killed in battle. If he fights well, he knows that he will meet his friends again that very evening in Paradise.

With a weapon and a little organization, any kid becomes a superman, especially among a bunch of unarmed civilians. If he is lucky, he will grow to the size of a man still with the brain of a teen-age gangster.

Hitler's first thugs were probably like this. They got their blood tests by beating up Jewish merchants and wrecking their shops. This action was necessary 'to rid the Fatherland of inferior people who were responsible for most of its troubles.'

As long as a young soldier truly believes that he is better armed, better trained, better organized and better supplied than the enemy, he is not too hard to lead and keep motivated. However, what if every German house in the 1930s had a reserve veteran of World War I, with his uniform, boots, rifle and ammunition like the houses of the citizen/soldiers in Switzerland? How much fun would it be to face 100 to 1 odds if the other guys had guns?

For thousands of years, every war lord and dictator has known that the first order of business is to disarm the people who must be controlled. The Samauri warriors of feudal Japan could control hundreds of peasants, because it was a capital offense for a peasant to even touch a sword, with the sentence of immediate execution. This is the reason the Japanese had to develop the empty hand martial arts.

Several years ago, while driving around in Guatemala, I saw dozens of men walking to and from work carrying machetes. Those big, cheap knives are primarily working tools, but they could easily lop off the head of an adversary in a fight. At first glance, it looks dangerous. But on second thought, there may not be too many fights in the cantinas if every fight has the potential for ending fatally.

In the late 1870s the Colt 45 revolver was called, "The Peacemaker." It was also called, "The Equalizer," because it made a little man equal to a big man in a fight. It would almost make an old buzzard equal to a young punk. Those were tough times before there were enough lawmen in the West to keep the peace, but they would have been a lot tougher if only the outlaws carried guns.

I have several guns which I inherited from my father, and I can shoot them accurately, but I really don't like them. I don't even like them on policemen, but I know they are necessary. I would hate to see the U.S.A. become again so lawless that it would be necessary for everyone to carry a gun. But I know from reading history that we must never give up our right to do so, regardless of how responsible our government seems to be at the moment. Power corrupts...and absolute power corrupts absolutely.

We must not even yield to the temptation to have all firearms registered with the police. A list of the addresses of all the firearms in town is all that's needed to round up the guns of all the law-abiding citizens in one day.

We must give up the idea that we can pass enough laws to make everyone safe. We may have to fight again to preserve our freedom, and the surest way to lose our freedom is to give up our ability to fight for it.

Remember Plato: "Only the dead have seen the end of war." Those same people are also absolutely safe.

Your Vote Counts

I am ashamed of myself for losing my temper and walking out of a political meeting where I might have been able to do some good.

Since I will have to live with these people, it might be better not to say what county and what party. I suspect a similar story could be written about any of them.

The meeting was called for a Saturday morning, and I dashed over there without a shave or shower to be sure that Sherron and I would have an opportunity to be heard.

A platform committee had prepared 14 pages covering 58 resolutions to be approved or rejected by the convention. The vast majority of these resolutions called for vigorous government intervention in matters that seemed to me to be better left to individual and private choices. They were balanced in one sense...." Complete freedom of choice for one group, and government regulation of the other group."

I took some comfort in the idea that the other people there seemed to be normal and responsible, and they would surely reject most of this hogwash when it came to a vote.

Just to be sure that one more reasonable person was there, I decide to hang around and help, make grass roots democracy work.

I accepted a position on the platform committee to review the last proposals received before the deadline and work them into the agenda. These turned out to be a refreshing change from the earlier material, and I gladly helped edit them into a form which would provide an alternative to the emotional and meddlesome planks on the original agenda.

When the meeting reconvened after lunch, we were told that the meeting had to end by 4:45...just two hours for debate on more than sixty items.

The first hour was devoted to splitting hairs and making minor changes to the first seven items, but all passed over some minor opposition.

Then, since we obviously could not possibly finish at that pace, the next items were considered as a unit. They were generally acceptable, and although there were two I would have voted against individually, the package was more good than bad.

Three fairly reasonable items on private and home schooling were passed, but then three requirements for minimum educational standards were loudly defeated over opposition. Not too bad for Libertarians, but a big score for religious freaks, and a shocker for supposed moderates.

A couple more easy items were passed, and we bogged down in some stuff that nobody cared too much about.

Then with less than ten minutes to pumpkin time, the swoop fell. (Remember the fell swoop...or was it a swell foop?...Oh well....)

Nineteen religious items that would have made the Ayatollah Khomeini proud were proposed to be considered as a unit. It looked to me like a chance to vote the whole sorry mess out at one time, but either the chairman was confused or he was part of the plan. When the smoke cleared, everything was passed without a single dissenting vote.

I was amazed, appalled, and almost nauseated to realize that I was only one of a whole auditorium full of fools...possibly one group of fools making victims of the other fools.

I couldn't take it. I walked out without waiting to learn the fate of the resolutions near the end of the agenda that I had worked on. It was obvious that the meeting was packed and stacked, and there was not going to be any effective debate with a single minded majority. Incidentally less than half of the authorized number of delegates were there.

Folks, this is grass roots democracy at work...less than a hundred narrow minded activists claiming to represent fifty thousand voters.

The vast majority of the people who take no active part in politics are almost as guilty as the people who don't vote. As it is, any gang that understands the system and is willing to work the system, can take over the government. It happened in Germany in 1930s. If we let this kind of thing continue, we deserve the kind of government we are going to get.

If you go to the polls and vote for the lesser of two evils, you are still voting for evil.

Most of the candidates are better than the parties they claim to represent, but they have to court the party's active members before they can even be nominated.

Most of our elected officials are far more moderate and reasonable than they claimed to be when they were running for office.

Apparently not many people vote a straight party ticket, and as the old German Sprichwort says. "Die Suppe wird nicht zu heiss gegessen wie sie gekocht wird." (The soup is never eaten as hot as it is cooked.)

I hope so. I can't take it according to the recipe.

All Men Are Not Equal

Even if they are right, I get tired of the women in my life calling me a "Male Chauvinist", so I looked it up. Here it is:

CHAUVINISM–Excessive and unreasonable NATIONALISM mingled with XENOPHOBIA. The word is derived from the name of Nicolas Chauvin, a Napoleonic soldier famous for his simple minded devotion to Napoleon, and applied by analogy to all extreme intellectual positions held by defenders of a particular set of interests.

Aside from the probability that Nicolas was not female, I find it hard to make the connection.

I also had to look up XENOPHOBIA, "The condition of disliking individuals or groups thought of as foreign. The 'group' may range in size from an entire continent (as with anti–American or anti–European) to a neighboring family of immigrants (or even migrants from another part of the country, if regarded as intrusive); and the dislike can range in intensity from a normally controlled awareness of preference to an abnormal state of pathological fear and anxiety."

Still no help. I like women. I married two of them, and I raised three daughters, with a considerable amount of tender loving care in all cases. I was a Women's Libber long before there was a name for it. Since the time my first daughter was born, I was repelled by the idea of turning her or her sisters over to some slob whose only qualification was the ability to drain a beer standing up.

If we were superior beings from another planet or gods cultivating the human race for our own benefit, we would castrate and eat the vast majority of the males. Only those which exhibited special ability as soldiers, construction workers, editors and writers, etc. would be kept for breeding. And since each male could only service a few dozen females, we would keep a large number of colonies separate to concentrate each colony on the development of a certain desirable trait.

In these colonies the babies would be watched carefully to see that they developed the target characteristics, and if not their daddy would be killed and eaten. Even a successful daddy would be replaced by one of his sons long before he was ready to retire voluntarily. Only the obviously defective females would be weeded out. God must have decided that Adam, Noah and Abraham were the kind of studs He wanted to propagate.

In a free society hardly any man would voluntarily eliminate himself from the breeding process, and most would fight any other man who tried to make the decision for him.

Apparently the gang on our planet noticed several thousand years ago that the babies turned out to be roughly equal in boys and girls. A lot of fighting could be saved if a new rule was adopted whereby each boy was awarded one girl, without regard to their qualifications. They gave up any hope of improving the breed in exchange for a little peace on earth. (Check spelling of peace.)

There, gentle reader, you have the origin of the idea, "That all men are created equal."

A Memorial To Vivian Samuelson Smith
June 17, 1990

A few years ago the Georgetown Railroad drilled dozens of wells looking for water for their largest customer. Most were dry or nearly so, but five were real gushers, producing 500 gallons per minute or more. However, only one was in a convenient location, so the others were capped off and filed for future reference.

Vivian Smith, wife of the publisher of the Brady Standard and a columnist in her own home town, is a part-time rancher and expert on pecan trees. She hated to think about all that water only a hundred feet down not being used to produce something to eat.

So Vivian arranged for Ann McKay, Georgetown Railroad's greenest thumb to visit several pecan orchards around San Saba and learn how the experts were planting and irrigating pecan trees.

By mid-winter Ann had gathered a gang of electricians, well diggers and ditch diggers, plumbers and nurserymen and worried them until they had a mile of pipe and sprinklers marching across Georgetown Railroad's land southeast of Georgetown. These guys know from first-hand experience that, "On the eighth day God created Woman, and since then nobody has rested."

Incidentally, Ann didn't just tell the men what to do. She got more dirt and sweat and insect bites than anybody else.

By the end of February 130 trees were planted, 40 feet apart along the south side of a 100 foot right-of-way that Georgetown Railroad is donating to Williamson County for the first part of a proposed high-speed loop around the southeast of Georgetown. Eventually this will connect Interstate 35 to Highway 29 and allow trucks and trains to quit barging through the oldest and prettiest part of Georgetown.

For several months there was one tree that couldn't seem to get the idea, but last month it put out some leaves to bring Ann McKay's batting average up to a thousand. That's what you mean by a "green thumb."

Although Ann did most of the work, she is just a young chick compared to Vivian Smith, who celebrated her 79th birthday on June 17th this year. Since it was Vivian's idea in the first place, the project was named in her honor. A granite stone about two feet wide and a foot high was placed at each end of the line of trees and inscribed, "Vivian Samuelson Smith Pecan Grove."

How To Fly A Model Glider

My newest hobby has given me a badly needed dose of humility. I have been certified by the Federal Aeronautics Administration as competent to fly a single or multi-engine airplane, helicopter, or glider, on land or sea, night or day, in fair weather or foul, and I have been practicing for 46 years.

However, I have also been certified IN-competent to fly a three pound radio controlled model airplane in the most convincing way...by a long series of non-fatal crashes.

I almost gave up before I discovered the Georgetown Aero Modelers Association. In order to use their flying site, I had to pay $36 dues and join the Academy of Model Aeronautics for another $40. The A.M.A. provides a million-dollar insurance policy to cover the possible damage my incompetence or bad luck might inflict on others. But the big advantage of membership is that I started getting some help, and less discouraging experiences.

Boys as old as I am will remember the extreme difficulty, noise, and mess associated with model airplanes of the 1930s. Some of that is beginning to change.

My favorite change is the appearance of quiet, electric battery powered model airplanes. Although they are low powered compared to their noisy cousins, they fly more like real airplanes. They are so quiet that it's hard to know when the motor stops, but it becomes obvious when the plane starts to come down. Then you get some landing practice...ready or not.

I get a couple of dozen successful flights between crashes now, thanks to a lot of help from Brian Joslin, Joe Lake, Woody Erminger, Fred French, and John Castle, the owner of the Pit Stop Hobby Shop in Round Rock. They have saved me a lot more than the dues I have paid, and made the hobby a pleasure instead of total frustration, as in the past.

I believe I have found the best way for a beginner to get started. A glider is the ultimate for silent flight. Bigger is better up to about six feet of wing span, because it can fly slowly, giving the beginner more time to react.

Two controls (rudder and elevator) are more than enough for a beginner, but rudder only is not enough. Plenty of dihedral in the wings makes aileron control unnecessary.

A HIGH-START is a better deal than either fuel or battery power. A stake in the ground holds one end of a hundred feet of surgical rubber tubing, while the other end is attached to 300 feet of kite string. A little parachute at the end of the kite string is loosely connected to a hook on the bottom of the glider. When the rubber is stretched to about three times its normal length, it will pull the glider almost vertically up to two or three hundred feet...enough for a two minute flight.

I justify the time and money I spend by the exercise required for each flight. A 100 yard walk to pick up the parachute at the end of the kite string, then another hundred yards to stretch the rubber.

Every flight gives the pilot landing practice, and a beginner gets another 100 yard walk to pick up the glider, until he learns to land it right at his feet.

I have made ten flights in a half hour before going to work at 8:00 AM. That's a mile or two of walking...not much for an athlete, but enough for a fat, old buzzard.

The instructors who have been helping me are all excellent pilots, and I would not have got to the sophomore stage without them. However, none of them gave me a complete set of really simple steps that I have settled on by trial and error.

1. The glider absolutely must be balanced or a little nose heavy. The center of gravity must be 25 to 30 per cent of wing chord back from the leading edge.
2. A hand launch from six feet high at 15 MPH air speed will give a 100 foot flight and a landing going straight away from the pilot.
3. After a dozen successful straight away landings, the instructor should hand launch the glider toward the pilot from a hundred feet away. This way the pilot learns to push the stick toward the low wing when the plane is coming toward him.
4. Next, on the high-start launch, the pilot learns to make rudder corrections as soon as the glider starts to turn in the wrong direction...not wait 'till it is going the wrong way.

5. The instructor should take the controls BEFORE the flight is in trouble, just as soon as the pilot fails to follow instructions...no conversation...no debates.
6. Never depend on depth perception. Some sky must always appear below the plane and above any obstacle. If not, either get higher, or come closer.

There they are...six simple steps. Those and three or four hundred bucks (retail) will get you started in the ideal retirement hobby. It's much safer and cheaper than either flying full-size airplanes or chasing women.

The Power Of Photovoltaic Cells
June 17, 1990

In the mid 1960s I sold computers for IBM and later started my own software company. I noticed that every three or four years a new generation of computers came on the market, more powerful and much cheaper than the one before.

In order to demonstrate to my customers why they should rent computers instead of buying them, I drew a graph showing how the price of a machine with 8K of memory had followed a decreasing curve. Extrapolating the curve out to the 1980s predicted that computers would become unbelievably cheap, but that is just what happened. An 8K machine that filled a big, air conditioned room and cost $250,000 will now fit in your pocket and sells for $100.

Recently while studying the proposals from that time for a Solar Power Satellite, I drew a similar graph showing how the price per watt of photovoltaic cells has been dropping. If the rate of decrease continues, we could have electric power from sunlight at a competitive cost in around ten years.

Batteries are getting better and cheaper too, but not as fast as photovoltaic cells. I have been flying radio controlled model airplanes with battery-powered electric motors. They are a bit heavy and weak, but still amazing to the old buzzards who grew up with me in the 1930s.

For a couple of years I kept an aluminum row boat with an electric trolling motor on the beach at Lake Buchanan. One of the seats was a thin-film photovoltaic panel which kept the batteries charged up for frequent trips out to the sailboats moored off shore.

This year I used three panels like the one on the electric rowboat to replace the worn-out canopy on an ancient 36-volt golf cart. It still needs to be plugged in when the grandchildren come to visit, but it lives nicely on sunlight when it is only used for hauling laundry and kitchen supplies around the 50-acre Buchanan Yacht Club and RV resort.

My secretary, Ann McKay drives an electric auto to work every day and plugs it into a special socket in the parking lot. It runs on twenty lead-acid golf cart batteries for thirty or forty miles between fill-ups as long as she doesn't try to drive it at highway speeds. She is lucky to get ten or fifteen miles range at 65 miles per hour.

Based on what I have seen, I predict that batteries will still be an economic problem ten years from now when photovoltaics are dirt cheap, although I would welcome a pleasant surprise when Frank McBee announces the breakthrough he has been working on.

However, here is an idea I will throw into the public domain. It depends only on the development of cheap photovoltaic cells, and it is especially good for Texas.

Most people, who pay for electricity only by the kilo-watt-hour (KWH) don't know that the big customers pay in two ways, based on two separate meters. One meter shows the energy they used in KWH just like residential users. But the other meter records the peak demand in kilo-watts (KW) during the billing period. A big user of electricity might pay $10,000 per month for the energy he uses and another $10,000 the same month because he pulled a big load to cool his place during one fifteen minute period on one hot summer day.

A typical big user of electricity might be a shopping mall or a shopping center with a big grocery store. These places are frequently only one story, so they collect a lot of sunlight on the roof, which produces a big load for the air conditioner.

Although it might make sense to put up an extra roof, covered with photovoltaic cells, to shade the existing roof, it might not be big enough, and it would do nothing for the shoppers. As an alternative, how about building a roof over the monster parking lot. It could generate electricity while it provides shade for the customers' cars.

There are two ways to make money in business...by cutting costs and by boosting sales. Most businessmen would much rather boost sales, and what better way than to take customers away from your competition by providing shaded parking?

From the engineer's viewpoint, the beauty of the system is that it produces the most power at exactly the time when the demand for the power is greatest, eliminating the need for batteries. Also, there is no need to have an agreement with the power company. When the sun shines brightest, direct current motors could pick up the compressor load, letting the alternating current motors loaf. Reducing the peak demand saves costs at retail prices.

What a deal!!

Bureaucrats Find A Way Around Simple Low Bid

If you ask any bureaucrat what he needs to do a better job, the answer is always, "More money." If you ask a railroad man, he will say, "Less government regulation. Competition will prevent abuses by monopolies."

Here is an interesting case study close to home.

Every year, regular and reserve army units pack up their tanks and trucks and go to California where they can shoot at each other safely. The equipment travels on railroad flat cars to save wear and tear.

This is a good exercise that proves that the men and machinery are really ready for a war anywhere in the world.

A couple of years ago, Col. Mike Patterson, chief of plans and operations at Fort Hood, discovered that they were paying $3,750 per carload for the trip, while the units at Fort Polk, Louisiana, several hundred miles further from California, were only paying about $2,800 per carload. A closer look revealed that Fort Polk is served by the KCS Railroad, which interchanges with several other trunk lines, similar to the Georgetown Railroad, while Fort Hood had to deal exclusively with the Santa Fe.

Since Fort Hood sends 350 carloads on four round trips a year, the taxpayers were spending about two and half million dollars extra every year because of the lack of competition at Fort Hood. Yes, Virginia, Adam Smith was right.

In an effort to save the taxpayers a little money Col. Patterson decided to split the shipment. The rubber-tired equipment rolled on its own wheels to Waco where it could catch an MKT train and travel at a competitive price. The tanks, which cost so much to operate that "they should never move under their own power unless they are being shot at" were loaded as usual on Santa Fe trains at Fort Hood. We taxpayers did not save any money though. The Santa Fe raised the price for moving the tanks to bring in as much money as it would have received for the whole movement. Screwed again!

Last year, Col. Patterson decided to get some real competition at Fort Hood. He asked the Austin Northwestern, the

Georgetown Railroad, and any others within 75 miles of Fort Hood to bid on the whole movement. The trucks could again travel to the rail head on their own wheels, and the tanks would be carried by heavy equipment truck-trailers. The Southern Pacific and the Union Pacific were invited to bid on the movement, but were to be penalized by the cost of moving the war machines from Fort Hood to the new point of departure. Reasonable enough.

In order to be able to bid on the movement, the Georgetown Railroad spent several hundred thousand dollars building a new railroad yard to Army specifications a few miles north of Round Rock.

It worked like a charm. Even though the Southern Pacific decided at the last minute not to bid, just the threat of competition was enough to reduce the Santa Fe price to $2,992 per carload, saving the taxpayers $2,122,400.

Col. Joe Dale Morris, chief of defense movements for the Texas National guard, saw the new Round Rock yard and decided it would be even more convenient for National Guard shipments. The local bunch decided to try again.

This year, the Southern Pacific stayed in the game and came up with a price which forced the Santa Fe down to $2,443 per carload, saving the taxpayer another $1,568,000. Actually the SP-UP-GRR price was considerably lower, because it had to beat the Santa Fe enough to cover the "disability" of driving and hauling the equipment 46 miles from Fort Hood to the new yard.

Taking it all into consideration, the new bidders would have saved the taxpayers another $21,412, bringing the total savings up to $3,711,812.

But the low bidders may not get the job after all. Col. G.H. Turner, director of inland traffic for the Military Traffic Management Command in Falls Church, Va., has decided that the "disability" calculation should be based on 57 miles, rather than the actual highway distance of 46 miles. This is still a pretty good deal for the taxpayers, but a raw deal for the local folks whose investment made it possible.

The local bunch has asked Senator Phil Gramm, who has been trying to balance the federal budget, to look into this case.

Water In Orbit

Make Room For Small Private Enterprise In Space

NASA is having another terrible year. They spent more than two and a half years trying to decide who was going to take the blame for killing a school teacher on TV. During all that time the Hubble Space Telescope was "finished" and waiting for a ride into orbit.

The taxpayers spent an unbelievable amount of money for rent on a clean, air conditioned building and dozens of technicians in white suits and surgical masks keeping it ready for launching.

My hind sight is as good as any trial lawyer's. It seems to me they could have cut a hole in the roof and looked through the new telescope at a few stars on some clear night. They may have had plenty of time, but they say they didn't have enough money.

It reminds me of a sign I saw on the wall of an old engineer's office. "Why is there never enough time to do it right, but there is always time to do it over?"

I have been an enthusiastic supporter of the space program ever since Sputnik. I used to wish there were some way I could get involved myself. One of my classmates from engineering school at Texas A & M, Hubert (Grade Point) Davis was the head man on the spacecraft that landed Neil Armstrong and Buzz Aldrin on the moon. Of all the rocket scientists I have met, Hubert is the most practical.

NASA won't be completely wiped out by the current series of foul-ups. They just won't get as much money from the taxpayers as they want, and that will be a good thing. Then they will need someone like Davis at the helm to show them how to get something useful done on a reduced budget. I keep telling him that he needs to help some politician get elected this year, and then get himself appointed. He says he is tired of dealing with the bastards, and he would rather live on Canyon Lake than in Washington. I don't blame him.

However, he has come up with the best idea I have heard for the proper role of government in the space program.

We don't need a sight-seeing trip to Mars right away, and there is some doubt that NASA could pull it off with unlimited money. We could use a series of Solar Power Satellites, converting sunlight into electricity 24 hours per day and sending it to earth by microwave. We will need it before it can be built, and before the earth's store of petroleum runs out.

The project is probably too big to be launched from earth, but 99 per cent of it could be built from materials on the moon, where launching is twenty times easier.

That means we need a mining base on the moon, and to get there we have to start with a manned space station in low earth orbit, preferably over the equator.

Although hydrogen is the most common substance in the universe, it is not in a form we can use. The most precious commodity in space will be water. It is fairly stable in a light pressure vessel, and with electricity from sunlight, it can be converted into hydrogen for fuel and oxygen for breathing.

Hubert has suggested that the U.S. government offer to buy a few tons of water each year, delivered in a suitable tank in a certain orbit about 350 miles up. Every few months a shuttle crew would go up to lasso the newly arrived water tanks, herd them into the water depot orbit, and give the whole string a boost as necessary.

The government's first offer for WATER IN ORBIT should be just a little lower than their current launching cost of about $4,000 per pound. But it should get lower each year as guys like Paul MacCready learn to beat the game. (Editor's note: Paul MacCready built the man-powered Gossamer Condor to win the Kremer prize. He then won another Kremer prize with a man-powered airplane flight across the English Channel, and his solar powered automobile won the race across Australia for General Motors.)

In order for Davis' WATER IN ORBIT plan to work, the government is going to have to get away from the idea that they have the only committee that can design the horse and stop throwing obstacles in the way of small private enterprise in space.

Notice the word ENTER + PRIZE. It is almost too simple. All we have to do is drop the bait in the water.

A Fate Worse Than Death

Sometime before 1321 Dante published his *Divine Comedy.* He may have thought it was funny, but many people since that time seem to consider it a fairly authoritative book about Hell. I don't believe Dante said where he got his information on the subject, but his description was vivid enough to convince a lot of people that things could be a lot worse than the pain, suffering and death that went along with ordinary living.

Thinking along those lines, an inquisitor could maintain a fairly clear conscience about having a few heretics burned at the stake. The pain would only last a few minutes, and there was a very good chance that the victim might sincerely call on God in the last few seconds and avoid an even worse situation for the next million years.

The incorrigibles who could not be saved by such extreme measures were hopeless cases, and were just being moved on to the next life a few years earlier.

Also, just watching a blasphemer go up in smoke would convince hundreds of spectators that it would be much easier to get along if they would just go along.

We moderns tend to think of inquisitors, when we think of them at all, as evil and misguided men in positions of power. Of course they were, but there must have been a substantial crowd of common folks who approved of what was going on. Even the boss of an army can't get much done if his officers and soldiers aren't willing to help him.

As long as the army and the majority were willing to go along with this type of revival in the Church, the others had to pretend to go along, or keep quiet, or leave. Some of those who left were the first Americans to join the natives who were already here.

When the new Americans got around to writing their Constitution, the auto-da-fe was fresh in their minds, and might still have been accepted in Europe and the Spanish parts of America. Our bill of rights comes down pretty heavily on freedom of speech and religion, which makes blasphemy and heresy clearly no concerns of the government.

However, in using the words, "To promote the general welfare," they opened another can of worms. Maybe they didn't realize that the republic they had created would turn into a democracy in less than two hundred years.

Now almost anything can get through Congress if it seems to promote the general welfare. It could be helpful if an Act of Congress were just a general consensus on what is good and what is bad for the general welfare, but we want to be sure that the good happens and the bad doesn't. So the really troublesome things that come out of Congress make the good mandatory, and the bad criminal, and provide for fines and jail terms for those who don't agree with the majority of the congressmen.

It wouldn't be so bad if the public had complete faith and trust in Congress, and would automatically go along with whatever was run up the flagpole. Since that is not the case, it is necessary to create a bureau to enforce each new law and appropriate a few million bucks to cover their expenses, whether the money is in the bank or not. After all, the purpose is to promote the general welfare. We can't let money stand in the way of the general welfare.

The first items for general welfare were not too expensive. In order to build roads for the mail carriers, a few trees had to be cut down and sawed into boards for building bridges. Keeping a federal marshall or a sheriff in a frontier town was obviously worth the few cents it cost the average taxpayer. Fires were fought by volunteers having more fun with less danger than they had fighting Indians.

But Congress and the legislatures kept on meeting, and as someone said, "No one's life or property is safe when the legislature is in session. Every year thousands of bills are introduced, and hundreds of new laws are passed. We very seldom see any laws repealed. Outdated laws are still sometimes useful. If you can't convict a gangster of murder, you can still lock him up for breaking some law that is not generally enforced."

Notice the term, "enforced." It comes from the word, "force." The people we taxpayers hire to enforce the laws we pass are generally allowed to carry guns. That makes it hard to argue with them, even when they are wrong.

The more laws we pass to promote the general welfare, the more thugs we have to hire to enforce the laws, and the more we have to be taxed to pay for it all. When the taxes get higher than we are willing to pay cheerfully, we have to hire some more thugs to collect the taxes. The most dreaded inquisitors in modern times are the agents of the internal revenue service.

So we have just about completed the circle in a little over two hundred years. Our modern inquisitors insist that we salute the flag, profess our faith in the general welfare, and pay our tithes, except that the modern tithe is more like a third.

We may have escaped the modern blasphemy law which would make it a crime to desecrate the flag, but there is much more to be done. We have to keep fighting. There is no new world where we can go now.

Threaten The Best To Make Them Serve

Back when I was having female trouble, I was an instructor and tow pilot at the Black Forrest Gliderport, about 20 miles east of Pikes Peak. I learned that summer that I could get along beautifully with no newspaper, no telephone, and no TV.

This weekend, on my 4,400th day without watching TV, I finished reading Robert A. Caro's second book on Lyndon Johnson, *Means of Ascent*, published by Alfred A. Knopf. I read the first in the series, *The Path to Power*, about a year ago. This is an election year. You don't have time to wait for the movie version to appear on TV. Read it now.

Caro mentions several people I knew personally and many more that my father knew. When I was just a little kid, I learned from my Dad that "politician" is a dirty word. Pop didn't tell me why, but Robert Caro did.

He has been doing research on Lyndon Johnson for more than fourteen years, and there is no doubt that he has been very careful in his work. Almost one-fifth of the second book, 94 pages, is devoted to a bibliography and to a long narrative about his sources of information. He has personally talked to dozens and perhaps hundreds of people who knew Johnson well and helped him in his career. I have no doubt that he has accurately reported what he learned.

I don't know what Caro expected when he began his probe into the career of the master politician of the twentieth century, but he gives the impression that he is horrified by Johnson's disregard of principles and his willingness to do absolutely anything to get elected. Caro's writing is good enough to carry me along with him in an orgy of disgust.

I only met Lyndon Johnson once at a lobbying affair in Washington back in the late 1950s, and the meeting was nothing more than a handshake and a few words along with dozens of other people. Someone told me at the time that Johnson was a master of the "triple switch," that is, he could shake hands with one person, be talking to another, and looking at a third person all at the same time. That's what he was doing when I met him.

Since I have been reading Caro's books, I have asked several older people what they thought about Johnson. Ex-governor Preston Smith's answer is typical. "He did a lot of good for Texas."

I have been almost totally naive about politics. I hope to get a little smarter as I get older.

A politician's first duty is to get elected. Then because nearly all of the power in our legislative bodies is based on seniority, his next duty is to get re-elected. If as a matter of principle, a legislator refuses to use the taxpayers' money to buy votes, he will probably not be a member in the next session. As my friend, Rex Titsworth says, putting his hand over his heart, "It's the American way."

There have been some men of principle elected to high office. Caro is particularly impressed by Sam Rayburn and Coke Stevenson. Certainly there have been many more, and some are still in office. However, if you are trying to select a man to get a fair deal for your district or your state in an organization that is loaded with lying, scheming con men, all trying to buy votes in their own territory and planning to send the bill to you and your neighbors, who is likely to do the best job for you?

Lyndon Johnson had a perfect instinct for politics. He learned how it was done, and then did it, better than anybody had ever done it before. Caro thinks he bent the rules completely out of shape. I suspect he was just slicker at it than his contemporaries in Louisiana.

Johnson was also probably the hardest working man we have ever sent to Washington. He insisted that every letter be answered, and he and his staff would do anything in their power to get the best deal possible out of the bureaucrats for the people he represented. Before he went to Washington he was the hardest working and most effective school teacher Cotulla ever had, and he apparently never let up for the rest of his career.

It will not surprise me at all if Caro's third book on Johnson tells how he arranged the assassination of John Kennedy. Many of the Old Testament kings came into power by killing their brothers and fathers. It certainly would not be anything new.

If we want to be governed by a more honorable type of leader, we are going to have to change the system, and even more, to change our expectations of it.

First, we must quit selling our vote to the highest bidder. We must get away from the idea that if we don't take a government handout, someone else will get it.

Next, we must quit thinking that anything wrong, anywhere in the world, can and must be corrected by spending taxpayers' money.

Next, we must quit trying to get someone else to pay our share of the taxes.

And last, we must reduce the amount of taxes we pay. No matter how much we give, they will spend it all and ask for more.

A small government, doing only the absolutely essential things, will not be attractive to supremely ambitious men. We might finally be able to achieve Plato's goal of forcing the very best people to serve in the government by the threat that if they refuse, they will be governed by people inferior to themselves.

Self-Supporting Arts

July 30, 1990

More than 40 years ago Cynthia Sandahl lived in my neighborhood and played with my sister. Her brother, Charles, was older and partially paralyzed from childhood polio. He was pretty active, and later was elected to the Texas legislature.

When we were both grown but still young, Charles insisted that I read a book by Ayn Rand entitled *Atlas Shrugged.* I was very impressed, shocked and surprised, but also a little inspired...enough to read another of Ayn Rand's books entitled *Fountainhead.*

Atlas Shrugged is a yarn about a lady railroad president, who was probably a fictional self-portrait of the author, and two inventors. Hank Reardon was a non-conforming steel maker who was constantly in conflict with a socialist government, and John Galt was a free-lance inventive genius who organized a strike by many of the creative and productive people. The story is outrageous but well written, and well worth the time it will take to read it.

The other book, *Fountainhead,* is about an architect who also runs into trouble with a socialist government. This story is much more believable, and was made into a movie of the same name about thirty years ago.

Both of these books should be required reading.

One of the problems which Ayn Rand addressed might be of particular interest today...public support for the arts.

A publicly supported artist has created the sculpture or painting (or whatever it might be) which consists of a crucifix in a bottle of urine. I believe the title is, *Piss Christ.* Closer to home, Austin taxpayers have paid for an *Ant Farm.*

When the public officials who appropriate public money to support such work criticize the work, we hear passionate cries about "censorship" and "freedom of expression." When we try to withdraw taxpayer support from objectionable art work, we hear cries for independent groups of specialists in art and design to make the appropriate decisions.

These are solutions to problems which should not exist at all. There is absolutely no reason why an artist whose work cannot be supported by the public through ticket sales should be able to force the public to support his work through involuntary taxes.

To make a simple problem even simpler, the government has no justification for dealing with art work at all.

I am totally repelled by some of the trash that passes for music these days, and I can understand a cultured person's desire to expose the young people to the classics which have been appreciated by music lovers for hundreds of years. But regardless of how noble the motives may be, it must not and need not be done at taxpayers' expense.

Austin has a wonderful example in its own symphony orchestra, conducted by Sung Kwak. His series of four pop concerts this summer was an absolute delight for about five thousand paying customers at the Lester Palmer Auditorium. A little bit of classical fiddle music was sold in a mixture with dance music from the 1950s, an excellent saxophone quartet, John Phillip Sousa marches, and "Lone Ranger music." At one point the old folks were dancing in the aisles.

People like Jane Sibley, Marion More, and Sandy Perkins who want to show the young people what good music is like can make up possible cash losses out of their own pockets. Then it is up to musicians like Sung Kwak to gather the best gang in town and put on the best show he can produce. He is doing a wonderful job without any help from the taxpayers.

I believe Ayn Rand would approve.

Let's Get Independent Of Foreign Oil

August 23, 1990

"A kinder, gentler nation" was in one of George Bush's campaign speeches along with the famous, "No new taxes." By the time our adventure in the Persian Gulf is over, both will seem like bad jokes.

Every king needs a thoroughly evil, frightening enemy to make his subjects noble and patriotic, and cheerful about sacrifice and taxes. We found one just in time.

As long as the Arab war is limited to showing off the military power, it won't really cost much. The soldiers' salaries are being paid anyway, and the machinery and ammunition is already paid for (if you don't count the debt). The Saudis will probably be glad to fill up our gas tanks for free, or at least on credit. A few years of higher oil prices will be good for Texas. A few years of wartime taxes and inflation can wipe out the savings and loan debt, and our Texas weapons manufacturers will have a little more time to find another way to make a living.

After being burned by the Arabs twice in twenty years, we will be ready to do the things we have to do in order to be independent of foreign oil.

Austin people can call Southern Union Gas Company to learn how to make their cars run on natural gas and still be able to burn gasoline when it is available.

The City of Austin electric department can start to expand the photovoltaic system they have proven at Decker Lake.

We can use natural gas to pump water to irrigate sugar cane which can be converted to ethanol. It will run your car as is, but you will need to change a few plastic and rubber parts.

Dan Kubiak of Rockdale learned enough about alcohol to build a working plant ten years ago.

We can also run our cars on methanol, which can be made from natural gas.

Every house can use sunshine to heat water, using collectors that were developed in the 1970s.

We can share rides to work and save on parking fees as well as gasoline.

High school and college students can ride bicycles around the campus. It will improve both their health and their grades, and save daddy the loan payments and insurance.

School busses and local delivery trucks can save money immediately by converting to natural gas.

Thousands of wind turbines are generating electricity in California. There could be thousands more on top of every hill.

NASA could forget about their sightseeing trip to Mars and get busy on the Solar Power Satellite.

We can start to build the high-speed passenger train system to connect Fort Worth, Dallas, Houston, Austin and San Antonio. Texas' part could be expanded to reach El Paso, Harlingen, Amarillo and Texarkana. 200 mph trains use about one-third as much energy per passenger as airplanes.

For just a little more than Persian Gulf prices we can buy oil from Mexico and Venezuela, making it possible for them to pay off their loans from Texas banks. Otherwise the taxpayers will be stuck again. It's almost like oil for nothing.

We can quit acting like spoiled brats about the oil under somebody else's land. We are their best customer, and they can't charge us any more for it than we pay for our next best source.

If we are worried about the Arabs getting together to form a new Muslim empire like they had a thousand years ago, a war will just bring it on faster.

Let's leave them alone and get busy solving our own problems.

All of this will take time and money, but it will be a lot cheaper than a war, and not nearly as bloody. They are all things we will have to do eventually, and we should have done them when we got our first warning seventeen years ago.

Less Taxing Law And Order

Many people, especially those in business, will remember Parkinson's First Law, which is, "Work expands to fill the time available for its completion."

Snead's corollary is so commonplace that many people are not even aware of its illustrious author. It says, "Expenses rise to equal, or if possible to exceed, income."

I have spent a few days driving around Colorado with Chris Mealy, who has spent the last fifteen years dealing with criminals, first as District Attorney in Llano County, and later in Georgetown. He has served several years on the Texas State Board of Pardons and Paroles. This year he is president of the Texas Corrections Association.

Chris has observed a new phenomenon that has probably escaped the notice of most laymen. In this case the term "layman" applies to many people elected and appointed to high government office.

Chris is inclined to be a little windy at times, so I have had to help him distill this pearl of wisdom down to a memorable chestnut roughly equivalent to Parkinson's Law. So here is Mealy's Law. "Prisoners multiply to fill the space available to lock them up."

Political candidates like simple answers to complex problems. They know by hard experience that the general public's attention span is limited to what can be covered in a ten-second TV sound bite. It doesn't take long to tell the folks at home that you favor "Law And Order" and to accuse your opposition of turning dangerous criminals loose to harass innocent taxpayers.

Building more prison cells is an obvious solution to the problem, and it kills two birds with one stone. It provides places to lock up more "dangerous criminals," and it provides work for thousands of construction people.

In the last three years Texas has borrowed almost a billion dollars for the construction of prison cells, and the cost of operating these facilities will be about ten billion dollars over their lifetime.

If your goal is to keep a bunch of people working on tax-supported projects, it's not such a bad idea. But if you think it will eliminate the problem of overcrowded prisons, you just haven't seen the way the system operates from Mealy's viewpoint.

Whenever a real criminal gets caught...the kind that politicians build their campaigns around...there is always the possibility of saving the taxpayers a lot of time and money by persuading the accused to plead guilty to a lesser offense in order to avoid the possibility of being locked up for life. Incidentally the term "life in prison" now really means between seven and fifteen years.

These days there are seldom enough places to put the people who are sentenced every week. If the judge and the prosecuting attorney know that a cell is available, they can be very hard to deal with. But if it is going to be hard to find cells, they are much more likely to make deals which will just take thugs off the streets for a while and try to improve their attitude.

If you got a place to lock him up, you throw the book at him.

According to Mealy, if we could wave a magic wand and suddenly have ten thousand more jail cells in Texas, they would be filled up almost immediately. Texas now has about 45,000 cells, and in three years will have 60,000. But right now there are more than 10,000 prisoners waiting in county jails for a vacancy in the State prison system.

It costs about $50,000 to build a cell for two and about $18,000 per year to keep one prisoner...about $50 per day.

Here is a fairly new solution to the problem: Electronic monitoring of non-violent prisoners.

Possibly one-third of all the prisoners in Texas could be managed with electronic "dog tags" on their ankles sending signals to receivers connected to their telephones.

Usually a prisoner is confined to his own house for a month. If that goes well, he might be allowed to go to work, but be at home any time he is not working or commuting. He might also go to school or to drug or alcohol treatment...anything his parole officer believes would help rehabilitate him.

Electronic monitoring can be done for about seven dollars per day, one seventh the cost of keeping a person in jail with no "up front" cost of building the jail.

The gadget on the phone expects to receive a continuous signal from the transmitter on the prisoner's ankle. If not, the gadget phones the monitoring office, where a computer checks to see if he is scheduled to be away from home.

Before blowing the whistle, the computer calls the phone company to see if the service is normal. Then the computer operator phones the parole officer, who may drive over to the house and decide whether to call the police.

Once the prisoner tries to beat the electronic system and is picked up again, he goes to jail for sure.

A person in jail cannot do much for himself or for anybody else, so his family is likely to be on welfare, adding to the cost of keeping him in jail. If he is working, he can support his family and maybe even pay restitution to the victims of his crimes.

A parole officer can handle many more cases by electronic monitoring than he can by making personal calls, again reducing the cost to taxpayers.

I know I'd prefer electronic monitoring for myself, if it was that or jail, and as a taxpayer, I can afford a lot more "Law And Order" that way than under the old system. Let's look into it. Maybe we can avoid spending more money that we don't have.

Future Leaders In Space

I feel a little bit like Abraham. I have just made a deal to get my granddaughter into the first colony in space. This is no joy ride. She will have to be well educated in an essential specialty and trained as an astronaut. She will have to be in excellent health and about three months pregnant with her second child at the time of departure.

I have also arranged for Sherron's granddaughter, who must meet all the same qualifications, to go along. Since the Snead-Kerr-deSteiguer clan is not related to the Jordan-Smith-Samuelson clan, the colony will not be burdened with any early inbreeding.

I made this deal with Peter Diamandis, one of the founders of the International Space University, with whom I am also involved in a space venture.

Peter and his co-founder of I.S.U., Todd Hawley, who is now its president, are two of the most brilliant and productive young men I have ever known.

Peter and Todd are only 29 or 30 years old, but have already done more than most of the people I know in their 60s. While they were still in school in the summer of 1988, they organized the first ten-week session of I.S.U. on the campus of the Massachusetts Institute of Technology (M.I.T.). They raised more than a million dollars and recruited a faculty of 30 of the most respected space engineers and rocket scientists from all over the world. Then they found sponsors for more than a hundred students from all over the world at $10,000 a head.

I had the privilege of participating in the second session of I.S.U. in Strasbourg, France, in the summer of 1989. I helped with a study of an equatorial spaceport which had been a pet project of mine. Mikhail Gorbachev paid a visit to I.S.U. that summer, unfortunately not while I was there.

This summer's session has just been finished in Toronto, Canada. The university continues to grow and prosper with plans for a permanent campus to be established somewhere in 1992, the International Space Year. Next summer they will meet in Moscow. I hope I can take part in some way.

The faculty of I.S.U. which has generally been returning each year, represents the top players in space from about a dozen different nations.

The student body and the alumni now number more than 300 with an average age of 30, and are even more cosmopolitan than the faculty. They will be the future leaders of the space industry.

From my own experience as an inventor, I know that it is much easier to make something work than it is to sell it. Peter Diamandis and Todd Hawley have proven early that they can BOTH make things work and sell them to the most important people in their field.

I feel that my investment is relatively safe with them, and that they will eventually be the people who can give my granddaughters the opportunity to be the mothers of a new race of space-faring humans. Nothing is a sure thing, but this is exciting and may be a pretty good bet.

Truth Too Outrageous For Fiction

Sherron has been planning to write a travel column for several months, but I have kept her too busy travelling to write. She does all the packing, because she says I am color blind. It's not true. I see plenty of colors, but they don't make the same impression on me they seem to make on other people.

I grew up in Austin, from the time my father started the E. B. Snead Construction Company to build some steam distribution tunnels on the U. T. campus when it was still just 40 acres.

After the Korean War I hung around for eleven years, trying to help Pop make something out of Texas Crushed Stone Co and the new Georgetown Railroad. When I thought I had done all I could, I went to Houston in 1965 to help Tom Watson build up his little IBM outfit by selling computers to some bull-headed Texans. That was before Austin discovered glass buildings with tall elevators and suburbs in other counties.

By the time I got back to Austin, I needed help to find my way around. All this is an effort to explain why Sherron's first travel column is being written by her husband, and about some tourist attractions in Austin.

We had planned to take in the five o'clock show at the Live Oak Theatre and then eat supper at one of the restaurants who are paying the bills at the *Austin Weekly*, but I had found a new friend out at the Georgetown Aeromodelers' flying field just south of Georgetown and north of the Candle Factory, and just across Interstate 35 from Inner Space. All of these attractions are worth a visit, and not even as far away as Georgetown.

We were using my digital wrist watch for timing individual flights as we took turns launching my little glider with a long piece of surgical rubber tubing and kite string. We were having such good luck (or skill) that we never had to run down to John Castle's Pit Stop Hobby Shop in Round Rock to get repair parts. Naturally, with our watches being used as stopwatches, I didn't get home in time to dress for the play.

No problem. Sherron wasn't ready either, so we took a nap and almost missed the supper we had planned before the next performance. Driving through Austin with less than an hour to spare, I suggested that we go on to the play and find something to eat later. Sherron was agreeable as usual, but she started muttering things about being reminded of her first husband, so I decided not to press my luck.

We found a new place at about 34th and Lamar called Adobe. It was definitely not there the last time I went by. The first compliment goes to the architect. It is done with native stone in a definite Mexican style. The outdoor dining area is partially screened off from the traffic on North Lamar by banana trees and a wrought iron fence...a perfect tropical touch.

We told a charming waitress named Chris that we were in a hurry to get to a play, and she returned in about one minute with a couple of the best chalupas I have ever tasted. She said she had some influence with the cook.

We got to the Live Oak Theatre just as the last customers were being seated. The building is nothing fancy, but it is comfortable and tastefully done, and there is plenty of parking space in a lot between 3rd and 4th streets on Nueces. It's another thing that was not there the last time I rode by on my bicycle about 1946.

The play was *Driving Miss Daisy*, and I was disappointed not to see an old limousine on stage. What they had on stage was some cheap furniture, a couple of old telephones and *three professional actors*. Thomas C. Parker, who played Daisy's son and successful young businessman, would be a credit to any play. Miss Daisy, played by Jill Parker-Jones, had a pretty good Georgia accent, and aged convincingly from 72 to 90 in less than two hours.

In the mid-1960s my grandmother, Mary Brazelton, had a big Chrysler New Yorker which drove itself 70 or 80 mph because it made the road so smooth and the wind so quiet. The day she quit driving, she pushed the wrong gearshift button and confused the brake with the throttle and hit seven other cars in the parking lot. Miss Daisy might have learned from her, but the truth is always too outrageous for fiction.

The star of the show was Julius W. Tennon, who played the chauffeur. Being born black, he had no trouble with the accent. But being still young, he had to learn to display the Christ-like character of many of the old Negro men who grew up in the South before 1960. Maybe he has known more of these saints than I have.

The small cast and almost bare stage reminded me of a play we saw in London last year when Alec Guiness played the old Russian diplomat. It's nice to know that we have actors in Austin who can create the same kind of effects.

Just Keep The Oil Coming
Let Texas Railroad Commission fix the price

Most newspapers will not print material they cannot verify. However, this material which we received in an envelope with no return address was too interesting to pass up. The hacker who sent it (we'll call him Joe) says he might be in big trouble if he were identified or if he told how he got it. We leave it up to the reader to decide if it is true.

It must have started with some sort of request for help, because the first line was, "Good to hear from you. Always glad to help. What can I do for you?"

It appears to be more or less complete from that point. The other end replied, "That son of a camel has sent a bunch of pirates onto my land. I need to borrow your army for a few days."

"I don't know. That's kinda out of my territory. Isn't there some other way I can help?"

"No, this is serious. You better get some gunfighters headed this way. I'll tell the press, and just knowing that the Cavalry is on the way will slow them down some."

"Wait a minute. I'm not a king, you know. I've got to think about the voters' reaction to another war."

"They only vote one time each. With plenty of money for television, we can buy the next election. I've got more than that crazy Texan that wants to be governor."

"It's not just a matter of money. We've got problems here that I don't know how to handle."

"This is just what you need. A war is exciting enough to get their minds off their petty gripes. The enemy is a dirty old man who gasses women and children."

"You may be right. I'll get with my people on it and get back to you."

"OK, but don't wait too long. I may have to catch the next plane out of here."

The first record ended there, but Joe kept peekin' and pokin' until he found another record from a few days later:

"Hi. How are the wives and kiddos? Good. Good. My treasury man asked me to touch base with you about some bonds he's trying to sell. Maybe the word hasn't got around your part of the world."

"No, I heard. Trouble is, when my neighbor had to bug out, his income stopped, so he's not buying much for a while. The new proprietor doesn't want your paper, and my bunch is hanging loose. What have you done about the army?"

"I've been on the phone trying to round up some international support for your cause. I'm not getting much."

"That won't get it. Listen, I'm the only friend you've got left over here, and my gang can't hold out a week. How would you like for all of the rest of your banks to go broke?"

"I see what you mean. I'll get right on it."

There is another break of a few days, but Joe did find the next exchange between these two correspondents:

"How does it look back over your shoulder?"

"The first little bunch got here just in time. They slowed them down and let 'em know it's not gonna be a walkover. Just keep 'em comin'. There's not enough here for a real fight."

"You don't know what this is costing. Even if you buy the bonds, we can't afford the interest. We're diggin' too deep a hole."

"Look, money don't mean nothin' to us, especially if we're about to lose it all. We'll fill your gas tanks, feed the guys, and give 'em enough water for a bath every week. The rest is the best training exercise they've ever had, and it won't cost you a thing."

"Aren't you worried about all those GI's corrupting your gals?"

"Hey, you don't think I go by all that stuff, do you? I need the mullahs to keep the herd in line until I can get 'em all educated. Since my daughters came back from Radcliff I can't even keep a handle on my own women. Your boys will teach my girls more than they can learn in four years in Boston, for a lot less money."

"OK, but what if they start shooting? My gang won't stand for gettin' their boys home in body bags."

"Don't worry about it. The best way to stop a fight is to be ready for one. After a few months of threats and bluffing, you can replace the regulars with convicts who have a choice of goin' to jail or goin' to war. The French have been doin' that for a hundred years. Then I'll buy all the machinery you want to leave here, just as soon as your guys show mine how to run it."

"Say, that's a good deal. I've been wanting to buy some new stuff anyway, but how are you gonna keep it runnin' in all that sand?"

"We'll just buy spare parts from your hardware factories, using the money we'll make from sellin' oil to the Germans and Japs."

"It's sounding like a better deal all the time. Do you think you can keep the oil comin' at a good price?"

"I know we can. We're gonna let Texas join OPEC and put the Railroad Commission in charge of price fixin'."

The Lesser Of Two Evils Is Still Evil

Near the middle of the October 15th issue of *Time* is an article by Stanley W. Cloud with the headline, "Who Deserves the Blame?" It has an eye-catching red line across the page showing graphically how the portion of the national debt owed by every man, woman and child has more than tripled from $3,989 in 1980 to $12,409 today.

The first half of the article recites the sins of the Democrat controlled Congress and the Republican administration, but Cloud recognizes that a politician cannot stay in office unless he does what the voters demand. He says, "...in the end the American people must accept responsibility for what is happening.... Too many voters have allowed themselves to be seduced by the notion that they can have their goodies from government with no increase in price. A mighty military, Social Security, Medicare, farm subsidies, poverty programs, housing, highways, bridges, clean air, clean water, veterans' benefits—the whole great panoply of federal involvement in American life—must, like everything else, be paid for. ...Anyone who thinks—or promises—otherwise is either a dupe or a snake-oil salesman."

Earlier in the article, Cloud notes a mood building among the voters to, "throw the bums out." He says, "voters...could do worse than simply elect challengers across the board. They could, as a matter of fact, do a lot worse; they could return all the incumbents for another term of madness."

Every day someone, completely disgusted with the way some campaign is going asks me who I plan to vote for. They'd like help in choosing between the lesser of two evils. I have to remind them that when you vote for the lesser of two evils, you are still voting for evil.

This year, voters may be surprised to see a third candidate for many of the offices. It will seldom be a well-known person, because they don't attract big money from lobbyists. However, you can be sure of one thing. They are opposed to the INITIATION OF FORCE for any purpose, government or private. In addition, they believe that people can solve most of their own problems, leaving the government to handle only national defense, police, and the courts.

Most of these wild-card candidates have no experience in public office. Their chances of being elected run from slim to none, but they need a few votes to stay on the ballot next year. A few more votes will earn government subsidies for campaign costs, giving them the same odds as the major parties. A few more votes will make it necessary for the major parties to make a few "deals" with these people who advocate less government and lower taxes. It could grow into a good thing.

Congressmen don't read much, but they do read polls. They are even more avid readers of election returns. A surprising number of votes for little-known candidates will have a strong influence on those who are elected. They will learn what these candidates stand for and make some changes to try to pick up the stray voters. These stray votes carry much more weight than just another vote for "more of the same."

So here's what I say to my friends who want help in choosing between the lesser of two evils. There are a few politicians I know personally and trust. I will vote for them. But in all other races I plan to vote for the Libertarian candidate.

Advertising Pays Off In Votes

This may be the most cynical thing you will read this week. It concerns money and politics.

If I were to register under a dozen different names and then vote a dozen times over town, I would be guilty of a crime and subject to punishment. However, I can effectively vote about 500 times in a federal election, and even more in a state election, if I want to.

They say that half of all advertising is wasted, and if we knew which half, we would cut it out. On the other hand, if the effective half gets enough results to pay for all of it, then advertising can still be a good investment.

It is asking too much to expect all voters to make a careful study of all candidates running for all the offices. All of us except professional politicians will be confronted by dozens of unfamiliar names on the ballot. If we don't just flip a coin, we will probably vote for someone whose name is familiar, even if we can't remember what we have heard about that person. We would be doing the careful voters a favor if we didn't vote at all in a race where we have no knowledge, but somehow we just hate to waste a vote.

Advertising can make the difference. If I have heard the name or seen the face in a favorable setting, I feel that I know something about that person...not enough to trust him with my tax money perhaps, but after all, I have never heard of the other guy. Bang, advertising pays off again.

Nothing is certain, but a reasonable rule of thumb says that it takes about two dollars worth of advertising to buy one vote. So, if I give a candidate the $1,000 allowed in a federal election, I have in effect voted 500 times.

The decisions made and the votes cast by elected officials can often affect us far more than the value of any possible campaign contributions. Even if we don't want any favors for ourselves, we may feel that it's necessary to offset the bribes we know the other guys are making.

Of course, a campaign contribution is not a bribe, but an elected official is much more likely to answer a phone call from someone who is generally a big campaign contributor.

Incidentally, campaign funds do not have to be spent if they aren't needed. If the polls show that a candidate is running well ahead of his opponent, he will save the money for the next election, when the opposition may be tougher. If an office holder gets so well known that he never has to campaign hard, he may wind up his political career with several million dollars of unspent campaign contributions in his war chest. In the past, and even for the next two years, an office holder who retires can keep his unused campaign money to sweeten his retirement nest egg. Unless Congress changes it, this little benefit disappears in 1992, but until then campaign contributions to many old hands look more like bribes.

Austin's Photovoltaic Power Plant
(Expensive now, but it will get cheaper)
October, 1990

A journalist can get his biggest thrill out of catching elected officials wasting money. Several years ago the Austin City Council decided to build a machine to make electricity out of sunlight. The only hitch is that it cost nine times as much as it would have cost to produce the same amount of electricity with a diesel engine or a gas turbine.

In this case I'm glad they did it, and I hope they will do it again, more and better.

Not too long ago a natural gas burning plant like the one at Decker Lake could be built for about $500 per kilowatt, or about 50 cents per watt. Modern coal burning plants like the LCRA plant at LaGrange cost about twice as much, about a dollar per watt. Photovoltaic panels, which convert sunlight directly to electricity without any waste heat, ash, acid rain or greenhouse gasses, now cost about $10 per watt.

But the price of photovoltaics is coming down fast, about like the price of computers have in the last 30 years. There are a lot of similarities. In 1960, a computer was thousands of vacuum tubes, resistors and capacitors, painfully soldered together by hand. Today more power than a whole room full of 1960 equipment is printed on a single chip of silicon smaller than a postage stamp. If it is touched by human hands, it is ruined.

Until recently, solar cells were made from fantastically pure and expensive single crystals of silicon, sliced into paper-thin wafers and soldered together by hand. Today some sailboats have their batteries charged by solar panels made of amorphous silicon printed on plastic. I have three of them on the roof of a golf cart. They are not as efficient as the ones made from the blue jewelry, but they are cheaper. Other more efficient, and more expensive, solar cells will get down to a dollar a watt by 1995, and certainly by the year 2000.

But, taxpayers of the city of Austin can do something to help the research and mass production if they are assured of a big market for their products.

I suggest that the city of Austin make a 10-year commitment to install one megawatt of photovoltaics every year. Only one contract would be awarded to the lowest bidder each year, but the losers would keep trying to improve their efficiency and lower their costs in an effort to get next year's contract. By the year 2000, we might have the largest and most efficient solar-electric plant in the world.

We have already started in this direction, and the results so far are excellent. Rather than just complaining, we would be doing something effective about our air and water, our domestic technology, our foreign trade deficit and our dependence on foreign oil. I call that a good investment.

Austin
Good Place For Global Campus

Three years ago I was in Brasilia trying to persuade minor government officials that their Ilha Mexiana, directly on the equator at the mouth of the Amazon, could be the world's best space port. I was also saying that they could advance their own space program by holding July and August sessions of a space engineering academy, using retired or vacationing NASA engineers for a faculty. Any place in Brazil is better than Houston in August.

I didn't know it, but while I was there, Todd B. Hawley and Peter H. Diamandis were holding the first session of the International Space University on the M.I.T. campus in Boston. These two young men, not yet 30 at the time, had already done what I thought would require many more experienced people several years to do.

I spent a week in the summer of 1989 with the second session of I.S.U. at the Institut de Louis Pasteur in Strasbourg, France. More than a hundred students from about 30 nations were being taught by dozens of experienced space scientists from all over the world.

The 1990 session was held in Toronto. The next two sessions for 1991 and 1992 will be held in Moscow, USSR, and Kita Kiushu, Japan respectively.

The first weekend in November I attended a planning session for a proposed I.S.U. NET. The idea is to create a "Global Campus" linking a permanent central campus with six other campuses on at least three continents.

Full-time satellite and fiber optic links would give students and faculty free and unlimited access to each other and to a space library. The library in turn will be connected to major specialty libraries, using their catalogs and collections.

These young people, the founders and students of I.S.U., will be the world's leaders as we move across the next great frontier, space.

Many Americans will ask why we should spend billions of dollars on space exploration while we have so many unsolved, expensive problems here on earth. This attitude is understandable in view of a long series of highly public failures in our NASA program. There are two answers.

First, NASA has been aging for 30 years. Many of the young fireballs of the 1960s have died, retired, or become expensive bureaucrats. NASA may be beyond overhaul.

Second, most of our problems on earth are a function of the exploding, potentially infinite, population competing for finite resources.

I have an almost religious belief that earth is the ONLY place where life and humanity exist, and that our purpose and destiny is to expand into the rest of the universe. There is more energy and there are more resources in space than we on earth have ever dreamed of. We are ready now to learn how to use them.

The people involved in the International Space University are the best and brightest I have ever met. They should be welcome in Austin, which is the best place I know, if you have to live and work in a city.

They will be looking for a location for the permanent campus to be built in 1995. Why not bring them to Austin?

The Time Has Come To Legalize Drugs

The applause was less than might have been expected when Vincent H. Miller, president of the International Society for International Liberty, announced that the San Francisco Examiner *had finally gone public in favor of the legalization of drugs. Americans are proud of their nation and their constitution. It is not easy to stand up and cheer when your elected leaders make complete fools of themselves as they did in Humboldt County, California this week. The* Examiner's *editorial is so clear and persuasive that we reprint it here in full.*

Ned Snead, Publisher

Now that federal troops have declared victory and withdrawn from Humboldt County, it is reasonable to look again at the war on drugs (in which this two-week operation was a mere skirmish). Any way you slice it, there is no denying that this politician-declared war has been just about as effective as the war on poverty, the war on crime, and the war on cancer put together, which is to say, a complete defeat for William Bennett and his warriors.

Let's face it: No amount of laws, no amount of interdiction, no amount of anything has reduced the craving for or the use of drugs. Drug prohibition has accomplished exactly what alcohol prohibition accomplished in the 1920s. It has enabled crime to flourish, along with its attendant violence. It has created a worldwide organization of dealers and smugglers who are getting rich by selling illegal substances. Organized crime makes an estimated $50 billion a year through the sale of drugs.

This policy is wrong. The craving for mind-altering substances is as basic to humans as the need for food, sleep, and sex. It cannot be legislated away, and armies cannot staunch it. The criminal justice system is grinding to a halt under the crush of drug cases. Prison cells cannot be built fast enough. One-third of all federal prisoners are in jail for drug law violations. The federal drug war next year will cost $10 billion. It is a colossal waste of effort, money, and human resources. At a time of pressing social needs, this expenditure is criminal.

It used to be that only hippies (remember hippies?) spoke of legalizing drugs, but in the last two years, a number of establishment figures have reached the same conclusion.

William F. Buckley Jr., Milton Friedman, U.S. District Judge Robert W. Sweet of New York, George Schultz, Mayor Kurt Schmoke of Baltimore, and others have said that decriminalization is the best policy.

The time has come to legalize the sale and use of drugs. Treat them all like alcohol, which is legal though its sale is subject to controls.

Immediately, the alarms go off. We've heard the arguments. "With legalization," drug czar Bennett says, "drug use will go up, way up." Not so, says Baltimore's Schmoke. "I believe that over the long run you would have decreased use." Who is deterred by the current laws? People who want drugs can easily get them now. They're sold on the street in broad daylight. Legalization can hardly make them more available than they already are.

Another argument is that legalization is an effort by whites to inflict genocide on blacks, who are presumed to be the numerous drug users. "That is ridiculous," says Kildare Clarke, a top New York City hospital official. "People who say that, prominent black leaders, don't understand that the real genocide is going on right now among teenagers, mostly black teenagers, who are killing each other off on the streets in a fight for turf and drug profits."

"Even if there were a slight increase in addiction—and there's so much addiction now anyway, with drugs being illegal—this genocide, the killing on the streets, would end. Children would not be able to sell crack for money. They would be forced to stay in school, get an education, and learn a trade."

There is no point in continuing the war on drugs. It has not worked, and it cannot work. It can be waged only with the kind of repressive tactics that were used during Operation Green Sweep in Humboldt County. A class-action suit charging civil-liberties violations has already been filed against the government in U.S. District Court here. And what did the government get for its efforts? Some 1,400 pot plants. Not enough to put a dent in the supply of marijuana. All anti-drug laws should be repealed. The war on drugs should be called off. Just declare victory, play "76 Trombones," and march out. It always gets applause.

Swords Into Plowshares

A letter to:
George Bush, President of the United States;
Mikhail Sergeyevich Gorbachev, President of the Union of Soviet Socialist Republics;
Boris Nikolayevich Yeltsin, President of the Russian Soviet Federative Socialist Republic

Gentlemen:

Three years have passed since I sent this same letter to former President Ronald Reagan and General Secretary M.S. Gorbachev. Although relations between the United States and the Soviet Union are becoming more promising, I am convinced that we can proceed farther and more rapidly along the road to peace in our time. This is the reason I am sending this letter to you once again.

For many years we have been trying to find a way to reduce the danger of nuclear war.

All of the proposals to limit or reduce missiles and warheads bog down in the problems of inspection to insure compliance. Neither side wants to take a chance on disarming without being sure the other side is not cheating.

We don't want a lot of Soviet officers looking into everything in the U.S.A. that might interest them. Certainly the Soviets feel the same way about us.

However, there is a way that we can be absolutely sure that any number of intercontinental ballistic missiles from both sides are made harmless and do something useful with them at the same time.

My friend, Hubert P. Davis, an ex-NASA engineer, has told me that most ICBMs are three-stage rockets capable of lifting a ton or more of payload into low earth orbit. This capability could be used for all mankind.

The U.S.A. and the U.S.S.R. could lead the world in an international project to build a manned space station, a mission to Mars, or some other worthwhile task.

My own preference is for a solar electric power satellite. A few dozen of these could provide most of the electric power needed for the future. They would reduce the possibility of fighting over declining petroleum reserves and eliminate the necessity for releasing huge quantities of carbon dioxide and heat into the atmosphere.

The cost would be enormous, but even so, it would be far less than the cost of preparing for a war that we cannot allow to occur.

Whatever project is chosen, if it is in space it will require a manned space station and many tons of materials and tools in orbit. Some portion of the freight could be hauled by ICBMs with their warheads removed.

A bookkeeper in orbit could simply check off the missiles as their payloads arrive at the space station. Partial credit could be given for duds, although they might be a source of national embarrassment.

An agreement between our countries would provide the opportunity for thousands of engineers and technicians to work together on planning and execution of the project. In the process, some of them would become friends, and some would even be married. After a generation of working together we might be less likely to go to war against our friends and relatives.

We don't have to start in a big way. All we need is to have a simple plan for a space station, determine a rendezvous orbit, and decide who is to furnish what. All the rest will come naturally; not easily, but surely.

The three of you are in a position to give something precious to your people. Please offer them this opportunity for beating their swords into plowshares.

Sincerely yours,

Ned Snead
(Translated into Russian by Claude Proctor, Ph.D.)
August 6, 1990

Support For The Local Arts Community

Judging from the phone calls and letters, I stirred up a hornet's nest with last week's column. I meant to compliment the Austin Symphony Orchestra and Sung Kwak's superb showmanship.

Unfortunately, I used a shotgun when I should have used a rifle, and wounded some of the *Austin Weekly*'s best friends.

I am a musician myself, if you can count blowing a trombone in the Aggie Band 40 years ago. I even played a few gigs with the Austin Symphony back when it couldn't afford a good trombone player. These days I travel lighter with a barbershop quartet called the Lakeshore Bums. I can even pass for a dancer because my wife, Sherron, can make any partner look good.

In general, I believe that government should be limited to the functions specified in our 200 year old Constitution, and I am particularly negative about taxpayer support for the kind of "art" that may be controversial to the loyal readers who support the *Austin Weekly* and our advertisers. Unfortunately, money which has been taken from all taxpayers must be distributed in an even-handed manner among all "artists" who have any reasonable claim to be exposed to the public before they have earned a public following.

Surveys show that our readers are a fairly sophisticated bunch, mostly living well above the poverty level. I'd like to encourage those who appreciate good art, music, dance, and theatre to make tax-exempt gifts to the Paramount Theatre, Mary Moody Northen Theatre at St. Edward's, Zachary Scott Theatre, Ballet Austin, Live Oak Theatre, and all the others you consider worthy. Incidentally, this is indirectly government support, but at least it is selective.

Better support would result from our readers buying season tickets. You can help even more if you attend the performance or give the tickets to friends when you can't go. I know from first-hand experience that empty seats are hard on a performer's morale. Also, if it's a good show, your friends can tell their friends about it.

It's going to take a long time for my articles alone to get the good old U.S.A. back to Constitutional government. In the meantime, I have no objection to some of Austin's hotel bed tax going to support the Austin art community. I hope the committee that hands out the cash has good taste...at least up to Aggie standards.

Support Fine Arts

I want the *Austin Weekly* to support the fine arts in Austin. We plan to announce every performance you tell us about. If you put on a good show, we'll tell folks about it. We reserve the right to warn our readers about the stuff we think they will find offensive.

In addition we encourage readers to voice opinions on the question, "Should taxpayer funds be used to support the Fine Arts?" Please, no hate mail...just your honest opinion as a taxpayer yourself. We'll keep it going as long as the mail keeps coming in. I'm looking forward to some excitement.

Women Executives Might Make World Better

I learn something new every day. The nicest little pearl of wisdom I have picked up this year is, "You can't buy an election." I have much more confidence in the voters now than I had a month ago.

This is an exciting time to be alive. Changes are coming so fast that I am in real danger of being left behind. Many of the things I have learned by long and hard experience are no longer true.

I am delighted that Texas now has a lady governor. She had to be a tough old broad to get elected, but maybe it is still true that, "The job makes the man," or in this case, the lady.

Ann Richards is in good company with ex-Mayor of Austin Carol McClellan, Mayor Whitmire of Houston, Mayor Feinstein of San Francisco, Margaret Thatcher of Britain, Corazon Aquino of the Phillipines, Indira Gandhi of India, Golda Meir of Israel, ex-Prime Minister Bhutto of Pakistan, President Chamorro of Nicaragua, President-elect Mary Robinson of Ireland, Mayor Lila Cockrell of San Antonio, Mayor-elect Sharon Pratt Dixon of the District of Columbia, and U.S. Representative Barbara Jordan.

The world might be a better and safer place to live if all chief executives were ladies.

According to the Book of Ecclesiastes, "There is a time for everything." I have never thought of myself as a Democrat, and I don't now. The men of the Republican party have made complete fools of themselves, throwing away their golden opportunities, and bringing about this time of change.

I will give the Republicans credit for two great accomplishments. They completely broke the Soviets by almost peaceful methods, spending enough on military hardware to almost break our own country. At least it was better than war. Second, they have done an amazing job of holding down inflation, by borrowing instead of printing money as the Democrats would have done. But here again the price has been almost too high. The inflation cure has broken all our savings banks, and is well on its way to breaking our commercial banks and insurance companies. It has also made it difficult to sell our products abroad.

Those were two terrific performances, but they remind me of the story of the Tom Cat making love to the skunk. He said, "Madam, I have enjoyed about as much of this as I can stand."

As things stand now, inflation is the only answer to our current economic problems. Fortunately, nobody has to take the blame. The Democrats can blame it on the Republicans, and the Republicans can blame it on the Arabs.

Inflation is a painless way to tax the rich. (Painless for the legislators, that is.) It does not require any specific tax on wealthy people. The working people take a little hit right at first, but within a short time wages will rise to cover the prices of necessities. Inflation will save the real estate market and the banks, because their problems are simply loans measured in dollars, and loans are easy to pay off with cheap dollars.

We can avoid going back into the same situation by truly insisting on "NO NEW TAXES" and expanding that to say "NO INCREASE IN EXISTING TAXES." Bureaucrats and others on government payrolls will insist that they need pay raises to cover inflation. Our answer comes from Nancy Reagan, "JUST SAY NO." Government service must again be an honor and a temporary sacrifice for people who have proven their ability outside the government. Those who insist on top wages for their efforts must find a productive job working for a taxpayer. Those who leave government service must not be replaced, and attrition will gradually bring the budget back to something manageable.

I would also suggest that we not make inflation a permanent thing. Several years ago the U.S. Mint started producing fifty-dollar gold pieces containing a Troy ounce of pure gold. They are worth a little less than four hundred dollars now, about eight times their marked value. A little more than twenty-five per cent inflation, which we could easily see in a couple of years, will raise the value of these coins to five hundred paper dollars.

If this happens, we can start making all new contracts payable in gold dollars, with each gold dollar worth ten of the old paper dollars. Contracts made before the change-over would still be payable in the old paper dollars. Any new paper money would be redeemable in gold on demand. Remember, one-dollar bills used to be "silver certificates" before Lyndon Johnson used all the silver on his projects.

Our new lady chief executives cannot do any worse.

Austin Weekly—Chapter Eleven
November 20, 1990

There is a story about two neighboring farmers, one obviously living poorly and the other living well. One day the poor guy asked his prosperous neighbor for the secret of his success. The answer was, "I go by the Bible. I let the wind blow the pages, stop it with my hand, read and do whatever it says."

A year later the poor guy had a new house and barn, a new car and tractor, and all the new tools a farmer could want. He had passed up the neighbor who used to live better than he did.

When they met again at the L & M cafe, the fellow who had originally asked for advice offered this explanation. "I just did what you said. I let the wind blow the pages of the Bible and followed its advice."

"That's good, but what did it say?" the other asked.

He answered, "Chapter Eleven."

That story illustrates the idea that bankruptcy can be used to take unfair advantage of honest creditors.

Chapter eleven and chapter seven refer to the most often used sections of the United States Bankruptcy Code. Chapter seven provides for persons or companies to go out of business, sell their remaining assets, and divide up the proceeds fairly among the creditors.

Chapter eleven is an entirely different process. It is used to protect a potentially profitable business from abuse by one creditor which might prevent the business from paying off the other creditors.

It is called a "reorganization for the benefit of creditors," and it has been used frequently in Texas and Austin in the last few years.

By order of a local judge, a business in trouble is allowed to temporarily stop payment of all old debts and given a few months to reorganize and develop a plan of operation which gives all creditors a reasonable chance to recover their investments.

Before the judge will approve the plan, it must be accepted by a majority of the creditors, and it must provide for the creditors to recover more than they could from immediate liquidation of the business.

The Austin Weekly Corporation is going through such a process now. The founders put together a high-class publication and built up a faithful group of readers and advertisers. Unfortunately, they began when Austin was approaching the bottom of its economic slump, and neither the advertisers or the investors in Austin were as prosperous as they expected. So for a year and a half, they spent more than they were taking in, going in debt just like their Uncle Sam.

Under the new management of Glenn Cootes, the Austin Weekly has cut costs and slimmed down to where they can turn out a quality newspaper for a little less money than their advertisers are willing to pay.

Unfortunately, many of the debts that were incurred during the build-up period are coming due, and some of the creditors have threatened to take legal action which would force the company out of business. It doesn't make much sense, because the only assets a newspaper has are its faithful readers and advertisers. If you stop publishing, they disappear, and none of the creditors get anything.

I am one of the people who has loaned money to the Austin Weekly, because I believe it can make money and pay back my investment in a few years. However, I am not willing to put money in so someone else can take it out.

Glenn Cootes' new team is doing well. They are already publishing the best newspaper in Austin, and by next year I believe it will also be the most profitable. My loans to the Austin Weekly are overdue too, but I am willing to give them a little more time, and even loan them some more if they need it. We have asked the court to stop the other creditors from trying to kill the golden goose.

The tough part is behind us. The rest should be easy.

Garbage As A Cash Crop

November 28, 1990

One of my favorite stories is about the college professor who gave the same final exam every year. He never had to worry about the students cheating, because he changed the answers.

This is especially true of engineering. I remember an instructor in an Air Force communications school saying that we didn't need to know about transistors, because they were very expensive, and they could only handle small amounts of power at low frequencies. Now transistors control electric locomotives and police radar, and you can buy a thousand on one chip for a dollar.

Even the technology of garbage is changing. I have visited some of the largest cities in India, Zaire, and Guatemala and seen the garbage dumped in the alleys where the poor folks and goats cleaned it up.

Americans may be sloppy about some things, but we want our garbage gift wrapped. We set it out on the curb a couple of mornings a week and expect it to disappear before we get home in the evening. When I lived in Houston Louie Welch was Mayor, and he said, "Everybody wants you to pick it up, but nobody wants you to put it down."

He was right. We don't want it burned in town, or even out in the country, because it stinks. We don't want it buried where it can pollute the ground water. We don't want it dumped in the ocean where it can kill the fish. We just want it to disappear without a trace.

Fortunately, we can still afford to be fussy about our garbage. The cost of this magic trick of making garbage disappear is ten times or a hundred times what it used to cost when there were not so many of us and when we threw away less. When Louie Welch made his memorable remark, Houston's cost of garbage disposal was rising from a couple of dollars per ton to seven or eight dollars per ton. Now we are paying ten to fifty dollars per ton, with new restrictions adding to the cost every year.

At curbside, household garbage weighs about ten pounds per cubic foot. A big truck won't hold much of that stuff, so modern compactor pick-up trucks squeeze it down to about thirty pounds per cubic foot...better, but still pretty light for transportation, and these trucks may spend half of their lives driving miles out in the country to a landfill.

Some cities have architecturally pleasing buildings in town where the pick-up trucks can unload into a machine which further compresses the stuff into bales like cotton, which weigh up to fifty pounds per cubic foot. This is a reasonable density for big highway trucks or railroad trains to move at reasonable costs. These same in-town transfer points can also be a good place to separate the aluminum, glass, iron, paper and plastic for recycling, but there will always be about a fourth of the stuff that has to be burned or buried.

What's left could be baled and wrapped in plastic...remember the gift wrapping?...and hauled by truck or train to somewhere it is welcome. At this point trains are a far better deal than trucks. A train can carry a ton three times as far as a truck on a gallon of diesel fuel, and train crews are at least twenty times as productive as truck drivers. That means a train can go at least three times as far for the same money, and cover about ten times as much area looking for a place where the cargo is welcome.

But welcome mats for garbage are pretty rare these days. Remember, "nobody wants you to put it down?" The usual thing is for a big company or a city or county to buy a farm and spend a million dollars or more and a few years getting all the necessary permits to bury garbage. Then, once a landfill is in operation, it can charge ANY price to dump a load. It's a hell of a good business, and with all the politics connected with it, an ideal business for a gangster.

I have done some arithmetic on landfills. At today's prices, a fill of baled garbage only four feet deep will pay the entire market price of the best Texas farmland for less than a dollar per ton of garbage buried. The garbage would be covered up every day with fresh soil four feet deep. The next crop could be planted less than a year after the soil is first disturbed.

Garbage could be the best crop a farmer ever planted, and the land would be in better shape than it started.

By this method, a city the size of Houston would only need to *rent* less than a thousand acres per year. The cost could be less than they pay now for monopoly landfills fifty feet deep, which nobody wants in his neighborhood. Lots of farmers would get as rich as those who found oil on their land

"You got it...You sell it...You still got it. What a deal!"

Cruel And Unusual Punishment

A few days ago an article got by this publisher and appeared in this paper advising the people who want to outlaw abortions how to organize effectively to put pressure on the Texas legislature.

Even if the people who want to impose their morals and religious beliefs were an overwhelming majority in this republic, they would still not have the constitutional right to do so.

More than two hundred years ago the people who wrote our constitution had fresh memories of the results when Spain allowed the Jesuits to use the force of government to achieve their goals. It was called the auto-da-fe, the public announcement of the sentences imposed on people tried by the Inquisition.

In the bad old days there was some crowding of prisons, but it was alleviated by the fact that most of the non-conformists were burned alive at the stake. The theory was that a few minutes of intense pain and the certainty of immediate death would bring most of the sinners around and save them an eternity of much worse punishment in Hell. Very reasonable, if you think that way.

Some of the authors of our Constitution did not think that way, so they made specific provisions in the first ten ammendments (the Bill of Rights) to keep the Inquisition out of their new land of freedom. Mostly, it has worked pretty well.

The "pro-life" bunch believes that babies should not be conceived just for fun, but if they are, those responsible should bear the consequences. That sounds reasonable, but it overlooks the fact that people who do one irresponsible thing are not likely to suddenly turn responsible when they become aware of the consequences of their previous irresponsible act. They are much more likely to go on being irresponsible and let society clean up their mess.

There are lots of unwanted children around, and most of them grow into unwanted teen-agers. If they are not remarkable people, they will keep growing into unwanted adults. Many of them will end up in jail or an early grave.

Not long ago a gang of enthusiasts who called themselves "Operation Rescue" was arrested for interfering with the lawful operation of an abortion clinic and charged with criminal trespassing. They hired a friend of mine named Bob Phillips who is a pretty good Georgetown lawyer. He managed to get the first hundred of the demonstrators acquitted, but as they kept on with their civil disobedience, the courts became less tolerant, and several hundred were convicted. Some spent six months in jail.

A little jail time is an expected part of the civil disobedience game, but since we are currently short of space in the jails, I have a better idea.

The next time a local judge has to sentence someone for trespassing around an abortion clinic, he should issue each of the demonstrators an unwanted baby. In order to avoid a really stiff sentence, the convict would be required to care for the baby until it graduates from high school and has held a steady, tax-paying job for at least a year.

If twenty years of hard labor is considered "cruel and unusual punishment," maybe we should not impose such sentences on teen-age girls.

Making Money Out Of Thin Air
December 29, 1990

At the risk of insulting some readers' intelligence, I would like to review the process by which banks create money, not by some banker's trick, but in the ordinary course of business. It is important, because the reverse process is going on now.

To keep it simple, we will assume that there is only one bank in town, and that most of the town's business is between the bank's own depositors. Then assume that some unusual money comes into town, such as a royalty payment to Farmer A for taking oil off his land. Make it $100,000.

Farmer A deposits the check in the local bank. If the bank is a member of the Federal Reserve System, it is required to keep a part of the money on deposit at the Federal Reserve Bank...for simplicity, let's make it ten per cent. (The actual rate on December 21st was 6.5 per cent.) But the rest is available to loan to other customers.

So the bank loans $90,000 to Farmer B for seed and fertilizer. The feed store deposits the money in the same bank. $9,000 goes to the Federal Reserve, but $81,000 is available for another loan.

Merchant C borrows the $81,000 to stock his store with local products, and his suppliers deposit the money in the same bank. $8,000 goes to the Federal Reserve, but there is still almost $73,000 available for another loan, which goes to Farmer D for more seed and fertilizer.

Again the feed store deposits the money in the same bank, which sends $7,000 to the Fed., leaving about $66,000 for another loan.

The process continues until the original $100,000 deposit has grown to almost a million dollars...all real money, because it will all be repaid with interest, except for less than one per cent average losses due to bad business judgement.

The money can be repaid with interest, because it is used for productive purposes. Without fertilizer the farmer's crops would be smaller...maybe not even enough to feed his family. With more stuff to sell, the merchant makes a bigger profit, and may have to hire one of the farmers' kids to help in the store.

The process will work even if a small part of the money is spent on vacation trips or paying off gambling debts, but not quite as well. The part that goes for taxes is a complete loss to the system, except for the government handouts that trickle back into town to buy votes.

Up until ten or twenty years ago Americans were so productive that we could afford to spend about 40 per cent of *everything* on government and still get by. The party ended a long time ago, but some of the guests still won't go home.

The Democrats' answer to the problem is to create more money. They could print it, but it is much neater just to lower the portion of the banks' deposits that must go into reserve. Cutting the reserve from ten per cent to five per cent lets the banks create twenty dollars out of one instead of only ten in the illustration above. It works as long as the banks loan money only for productive purposes, but if too much is available, they start loaning money to gamblers, and bigger losses have to be covered by higher interest rates. Then more money chasing fewer products causes the money to decrease in value...inflation.

The Republicans have shown us how to stop inflation. They keep the Federal Reserve discount rate high, and they don't print money to cover their deficits...they borrow the money. This pushes interest rates up, which is a good deal for people who have accumulated enough money to live off the interest. It's also a good deal for Congressmen, whose excess campaign funds are in the banks, drawing interest.

The trouble is that money loaned to the government goes out of circulation just as if it were paid in taxes. If you loan it all to Uncle Sam, you can't loan it to a miner who produces fertilizer. You may have stopped inflation, but you have also crippled production.

Then when a gambler can't rent his new office building, and can't pay off his loan from the bank, the bank can't loan money to farmers. The money creation process goes into reverse. When some real money disappears, all the bank deposits that were based on it also disappear. Now you have recession, and if it goes on long enough, you have depression.

What can we do about it? Not much. We spent the money, and now we have to pay the bills. The inflation spring has been wound up tight, and nobody wants to take the blame for turning it loose. But the Republicans have been lucky again. They can say, "It's not my fault. Those Arabs started a war and raised the price of oil. Now everybody salute the flag, and don't worry about your savings."

Texans are lucky, too. We don't have as much oil as the Arabs, but what we have is worth twice what it was a year ago. A little inflation will be better than what we have had for the last few years. Just don't count on your savings being worth much.

Experience Of Others Is No Teacher

January 11, 1991

Every man and woman needs to know whether he (or she) will be a hero or a coward when we come to the most dramatic and terrifying experience of our lives. For a man it is war. For a woman it is childbirth.

The men (and women) who satisfy themselves in war will be able to follow their better judgement for the rest of their lives without too much concern for the opinions of others. Most of the people who participate in wars are not killed, and the fate of individuals has almost nothing to do with their performance. It would be better if the cowards were killed, because otherwise they will be a burden to their neighbors for the rest of their lives. Among other things, they will insist on their right to dominate women and plant babies, and insist that their victims be required to bear and raise their babies in order to demonstrate their heroic manhood. They must be allowed to "make love," because it helps to keep them peaceful, but we must not require others to clean up the messes they leave behind.

Every woman must be allowed to bear one child in order to prove to herself that she is a real woman. If the process can be controlled by society, only those who demonstrate that they have the genes and the ability to create productive and self-sufficient offspring should be encouraged to produce more than one child. Incompetent mothers and the unfortunate children of incompetent mothers must not be an obligation and burden on the rest of us. The "love making" is necessary, but excessive reproduction is not. Contraceptives and abortions must be freely available.

Until a short time ago I thought it would not be necessary for the U.S.A. to go to war in the Persian Gulf. Now I believe it has been made necessary by past actions and by not doing "the things we ought to have done" like it says in the Book of Common Prayer. Both we and the Iraquis have produced more people than our natural resources can support. We have no choice now but to steal resources from others.

Only a few modern nations have managed to avoid war while their neighbors were fighting. Sweden and Switzerland are armed to the teeth but strictly neutral. Their rates of population growth have been almost nothing compared to our own and most of the rest of the world.

The other reason we must go to war is to give a new generation the opportunity to learn that war is not a game. It is the most horrible and senseless thing that humans do to each other. War teaches people that anything necessary to maintain peace is better than war. But apparently each generation must learn this for themselves. We cannot learn from the experience of others.

Prepare For American Economic Community
January 13, 1991

Time for another Snead prediction. Usually I predict things that happen, but too early. One of my best was calling the day that Lake Buchanan would run over the spillway after it had been down 30 feet in 1984. I said June 1st on the basis of sunspots, and it actually ran over on June 10th.

That was so long ago, and I have missed so many lately that my reputation has suffered. However, here we go again.

Next year, 1992, the European Economic Community will be in operation. The members expect to be serving such a large market that they won't need to court the rest of the world. In particular, they will tell us, the U.S.A., that we will have to play by their rules if we want to play.

We will continue to be unpopular all over the world unless we are spending money, or in rare cases where we are tolerated because they want to borrow our Army for a few months. We are envied and despised like rich kids who score about plus nine on luck and minus three on brains. That's OK. It's always better to be lucky than smart, if you have to chose.

But back to the prediction...we are going to need an American Economic Community. America, from the cold parts of Alaska and Canada to the cold parts of Argentina and Chile has more people with more elbow room and more natural resources than Europe. If yankees and Texans would quit acting like big brother, who can tell everybody else how to live, we might be able to get along with our closest neighbors.

The starting point is to learn Spanish. Far more Americans understand Spanish than English. Even the Brazilians can understand us when we speak what they call Castilliano. We don't have to worry about getting other Americans to learn English. They are working ten times as hard on English as we are on Spanish.

I'd like to do something about it "Right here in River City." I want to find a well-educated person whose first language was Spanish, to write a column for the Austin Weekly. It would not be directed to Spanish-speaking people. Almost everyone here who can read Spanish can also read English.

The column is to be an every week exercise for Gringos with interesting and memorable items about the way people think and talk south of here.

People who would like to become famous writers should send us a few columns of about 300 words each in Spanish. We will print what we like the best from several writers and let the readers tell us what they want to see regularly.

It won't be quick, but it will be easy and fun. By this time in 1992 we could have 75,000 folks ready for the American Economic Community.

World's Oldest Problem

Osmosis is a fairly well accepted scientific principle. A dissolved compound appears to cause water (and other solvents) to move through a semi-permeable membrane in order to equalize the concentration of that compound on both sides of the membrane.

As usual, anything so simple is not satisfactory for explaining the processes which take place in living tissue. Something similar, but more complex, causes the medication in a transdermal skin patch to pass through skin and enter the blood stream. We may not know how it works, but we know it does.

We also know that males and females produce slightly different chemicals which are generally known as hormones. Transdermal patches have been used to supply extra estrogen to post menopausal women.

Perhaps it is possible that females also require a small amount of some of the hormones produced by males, and that males need some of the hormones produced only by females. This mutual need might explain why sexual intercourse has been so popular for so long, even when there is no pressing need to breed babies, and in spite of many inconveniences and well known dangers.

The transfer of chemicals through the skin could be very efficient when body parts are in contact and supplied with large quantities of extra blood. The satisfaction derived from such contact could be partly due to the satisfaction of a very real chemical shortage which made the contact so attractive in the first place.

Certainly there are many other benefits derived from coupling, but the transfer of hormones for mutual benefit could help to explain the observed pressing need for body contact.

It could also tell us that restraint from intimate coupling any time there is no intention of producing babies is actually unhealthy. If we could discover exactly what is transferred and in what quantities, we might be able to develop a pill or patch to relieve the urge to merge. But until such wisdom is available to us, we may have to accept the natural system as necessary, and try to eliminate the harmful side effects.

Most of the risks of disease are eliminated by confining our mergers to one partner. The promises that priests try to squeeze out of us could be helpful if they were always honored. And they might be honored more often if married partners accepted the idea that married partners have no right to refuse to exchange essential hormones. The urge to merge should be satisfied at home.

However, there is another long term side effect which is a particular problem to civilization on a crowded planet. It could become essential to control this problem in the first space colonies where life support systems will be the most pressing of all concerns. The system, the society, the planet cannot accept responsibility for providing air, water, food, shelter, education, protection, and sewage treatment for every passenger who might be conceived during the transfer of essential hormones.

In addition to being a sentence of twenty years at hard labor for the mother, a baby is a burden on its family and its neighbors until it grows enough to contribute its share to the general welfare. Some babies are essential to carry the burden in the next generation, but too many could sink the boat.

When we are finally forced to get practical about this problem, we will have to start issuing (and withholding) licenses to keep and nurture what we produce. We will need more and better ideas than those I will suggest, but here is a start:

First, we must take full advantage of the various contraceptives now available. This would be encouraged by the assessment of a fee for considering the case of a pregnancy. The fee would cover the cost of processing the application for a license to bring on another passenger.

Second, the mother (and if possible, the father) should present themselves in person with complete pedigrees and the results of recent medical examinations. A prospective mother who is not able to bring her mate to the exam would have to pay a higher fee to cover the extra cost of evaluation, and as a penalty for poor judgement.

Third, the statistical probability of the proposed new passenger to carry his share of the load should be considered along with the planned capacity of the system to carry additional passengers. If the findings are unfavorable, the license should be denied.

If the parents are influential, and insist on their right to continue their line of genes in spite of an unfavorable finding, they should be required to buy a single payment life and disability insurance policy on each of them large enough to cover the expected cost of converting the new passenger into an effective crew member.

The license fee might be refunded to a couple expected to produce a particularly desirable crew member.

It should be fairly easy to get acceptance of rules of this kind from prospective passengers going to a new colony in space. Those who don't like the rules can stay at home. It might also be useful to try the prospective rules in a new colony on earth, so they can be modified and perfected before the first space colony is started.

Wrap-up
March 30, 1995

Someone has said that everybody has enough experiences to write a book. This is my second. I helped to write one about my father, Edwin Brazelton Snead, entitled *From the Ground Up*. Shortly before Pop's death I was going through a bunch of old photographs with my mother. We picked a couple of dozen which brought back memories with enough momentum to get me started writing. At the same time we made a list of some of Pop's old friends who were still living. Hildy Westerlund took the list and started interviewing. Most of the people she talked to suggested others who could fill in more details about Pop's interesting career. Then Carol Sadler took over and before she was through she had notes and tape recordings from more than 80 people. I was very pleased with the way Carol put it all together with excerpts from the interviews gathered by topic and story.

Hildy has done a similar job on this current book. However, she kept the articles more nearly in the order they were written, because I mentioned so many subjects in each article that they didn't fall neatly into subjects. I had to proof read every article several times going from draft to galley proofs. In a few cases my opinions have changed, mostly in a softer direction, but generally I have felt that I covered the subjects pretty well back when I was feeling more strongly about them.

Some of the subjects I wrote on are still controversial, maybe even more than they were at the time. I don't expect anyone to agree with me on every subject. Some people will disagree violently, and I ask them to take this into consideration:

> I never expect to run for public office again, so there is no chance that I will be able to force others to do things my way. One of the most valuable lessons I have learned is that I could never hope to please most of the people most of the time, and therefore I was not cut out to be a politician.

My next book, if there is one, will be an autobiography. It could turn out to be more helpful to others, because it will deal with the things I have done rather than the things I have only thought about. My career has been almost as varied as my father's, and I intend to throw in a few pearls of wisdom from my own experience, such as my advice on how to be a successful inventor. "You start rich and work your way down."

If you have read this far, you must be a friend or someone I would like to meet.

Sincerely,
Ned Snead